SPECIAL DRAWING RIGHTS (SDR) AND THE FEDERAL RESERVE

VOLUME 2.

SIR PATRICK BIJOU

Table of Contents

ABOUT THE AUTHOR

Sir **Patrick Bijou** is Senior Judge for the ICJ-ICC, Ambassador for the United Nations, a British investment banker, philanthropist, and a published author. Sir Patrick specializes in the debt capital markets, private placements, equities, derivatives and futures trading. He has worked with multiple leading banks such as Wells Fargo, Deutsche Bank, Credit Agricole CIB, Merrill Lynch and others, apart from trading on Wall Street.

He has over four decade's experience in the financial field and has worked with numerous prolific clients, including governments, banking institutions, and corporations. He is also a renowned author and has published over 21 books across several genres.

Sir Patrick was born in Georgetown, Guyana, South America. At the age of five, he came to Britain when his father obtained a scholarship to study and has remained in the U.K. ever since. Having been brought up in London, he spent part of his education in England and completed his education in the USA, where he obtained his degrees in Business Studies and later an MBA in Economic and International banking.

As a notable investment banker, he has also worked on Wall Street, and is a skillful and highly experienced Tier 1 trader in the derivative and bond markets, and he also established MTN desks within various significant banks. He became responsible for the setup of the MTN & Private Placement Desk and dealer functions within Lloyds Bank PLC, and was the first trader for Lloyd's treasury to increase the portion of self-led deals significantly from 4% to 32% in 2002.

Sir Patrick has tailored funding and investments for many different clients, including governments, banks and financial institutions, and has implemented over $16.B funding for socio-economic and humanitarian projects.

He has excelled as an investment banker and was awarded many accolades such as the Multiple Recipient, of the Wells Fargo "Valley of the Stars" award throughout his illustrious career. He was also distinguished by receiving the Wells Fargo "Circle of Stars" award, and was a Member of Wells Fargo's "Millionaire Club" and "Champion Circle". This further propelled him to then become the notable banker he is today. He was finally awarded his most distinguished accolade of all, a knighthood, for his services to banking and philanthropy.

His expertise is so profound that he was headhunted for a position within the International Court of Justice Redemption Department for his finance and international law proficiency to become a member of the Panel of Arbitrators of the International Centre for the Settlement of Investment Disputes. He currently sits as a Senior Judge of the ICJ-ICC. Sir Patrick manages to fit all these activities into his current role as Fund Manager for LWPCapital, and is also distinguished as being a U.N. Ambassador.

He is also a Global Ambassador for the International Rights and Welfare Association (IRAWA), and Ambassador of the Royal Diplomatic Club. In May 2021, he was appointed Ambassador by The Academy of Universal Global Peace USA as a member of the governing board/trustees and awarded The Human Excellency Award and Presidency of the Commonwealth Entrepreneurs Club.

One of his most significant career achievements was creating a line of credit for international supply chains and SMEs for the public sector and government funding through PPP. He also helped create the Contract for Difference (CFD) economic phenomena and credit leverage ratio concepts, regarded as hugely pioneering, which all banks and trading institutions have adopted today.

His journey into content writing has allowed him to become an exceptionally motivated and enthusiastic author and professional communicator, experienced in proactive campaign-driven and responsive communications.

His platforms are at Credit Suisse Geneva and DBS Singapore, where he manages high yield investments with attractive returns for selective high net worth clients.

"Coming together is a beginning, keeping together is progress, and working together is a success."

Sir Patrick Bijou

INTRODUCTION

The current global reserve system has three fundamental flaws: first, a deflationary bias as the burden of adjustment falls on deficit countries; second, inherent instabilities associated with the use of a national currency as the major reserve asset; third, growing inequities associated with resource transfers to reserve currency-issuing countries, enhanced by the high demand for foreign exchange reserves by developing countries, due to pro-cyclical capital flows and inadequate "collective insurance". Instead, the system should counter-cyclically issue Special Drawing Rights (SDRs) (to also finance IMF facilities), ensure "development" SDR allocations, and create a complementary network of regional reserve funds.

The debate surrounding the international monetary system has heated up in recent years through three different channels. Prior to the current crisis, attention was focused on the large global imbalances that the world economy had accumulated, as well as on the rationale for the massive accumulation of foreign exchange reserves by developing countries, which were part of that process. When the crisis erupted, attention shifted to the generation of international liquidity and countercyclical macroeconomic policies.

CHAPTER 1

Special Drawing Rights And The Reform Of The Global Reserve System

The revitalization of the International Monetary Fund was an essential part of this process. This led to the decision of the Group of 20 (G-20) at its meeting in London in April 2009 to inject resources into the Fund on a large scale, including a special emission of Special Drawing Rights (SDRs) equivalent to US$250 billion, which in turn revitalized this dormant mechanism of international monetary cooperation.

The third channel, the focus of this paper, is the reform of the global monetary system as such and, in particular, of the global reserve system. The proposal by the Governor of The People's Bank of China (Zhou, 2009) correctly placed this issue on the agenda (Helleiner, 2009). The biggest concern for the Chinese is the large potential losses to them, as the major holders of US dollar assets, of a disorderly depreciation of the dollar caused, in part, by the expansionary fiscal and monetary policies underway to combat the worst global financial and economic crisis since the Great Depression. Simultaneously with the Chinese call to rethink global monetary arrangements, the Commission of Experts convened by the President of the UN General Assembly on Reforms of the International Monetary and Financial System (Stiglitz Commission) also made a call for deep reforms of the global reserve system (United Nations, 2009b).

Both sets of ideas were taken up at the UN Conference on the World Financial and Economic Crisis and Its Impacts on Development, held in New York on 24-26 June 2009. In particular, paragraph 36 of the Outcome Document of the Conference states: "We acknowledge the calls by many States for further study of the feasibility and advisability of a more efficient reserve system, including the possible function of SDRs in any such system and the complementary roles that could be played by various regional arrangements" (United Nations, 2009a).

This paper argues that a better global reserve system can and should be based on an SDR-based IMF together with a network of regional reserve funds. The next section analyses problems that the current system faces. This leads to a closer analysis of the proposed reforms. The last section briefly discusses some complementary reforms.

Problems Of The Current System
Three Fundamental Flaws of the System

Since the collapse in the early 1970s of the "dollar-gold exchange standard" established at Bretton Woods, the global monetary system has been primarily based on the use of fiduciary US dollars as means of payment and assets denominated in dollars as the major form of foreign exchange reserves. Although other characterizations are possible, this system can be best termed a "fiduciary dollar standard". Since other national and regional currencies (the euro, in particular) compete with the dollar for this international role, the system can also be described but only secondarily as one in which alternative fiduciary currencies from a few powerful economies compete with one another as reserve assets and international means of payment. Flexible exchange rates among competing world currencies are another feature of the system.

The financial globalization that began following the collapse of the original Bretton Woods arrangement generated another feature that is more the result of the functioning of the global financial system but has profound implications for the monetary system, especially the fact that developing countries are subject to strong pro-cyclical swings in the financing, which generate significant macroeconomic risks (Prasad et al., 2003; Ocampo, Kregel and Griffith-Jones, 2007: Ch. 1). What this implies is that the integration of developing countries into global financial markets involves integration into a market segmented by risk categories, in which high-risk borrowers are subject to strong pro-cyclical swings (Frenkel, 2008). This is combined with the additional risks associated with the pro-cyclical nature of international trade, on which developing countries have increasingly relied. Some pro-cyclical features of international trade patterns, particularly commodity price fluctuations, were old but accentuated in recent years by the "financialization" of commodity futures markets (UNCTAD, 2009: Ch. 3). In the absence of a global lender of last resort, the risks generated by pro-cyclical finance and trade generated a defensive or precautionary demand for foreign exchange reserves by developing countries a mechanism that has come to be called "self-insurance", or better still, "self-protection" which has also contributed to the global imbalances (Aizenman and Lee, 2007; Carvalho, 2009; Ocampo, 2007/8, 2009; United Nations, 2009b).

As this paper will argue, the current global reserve system is both unstable and inequitable. Like all preceding systems, it lacks mechanisms to mutually offset the balance of payments surpluses and deficits of different economies (i.e., global imbalances) without adversely affecting world economic activity. Although most of these macroeconomic effects are contractionary, particularly during crises, the fiduciary dollar standard can also generate expansionary effects during global business upswings. Following conventional terminology, I will refer to these effects as the global "deflationary" and "inflationary" biases of the system, although their actual effects may be on world economic activity that is, on the intensity of the world business cycle rather than on prices.

More specifically, the system faces three fundamental flaws (Ocampo, 2009). First, it suffers from the deflationary bias characteristic of any system in which the burden of macroeconomic adjustment falls on deficit countries. As this was emphasized by Keynes in the debates that preceded the creation of the Bretton Woods institutions (BWIs), it can be called the anti- Keynesian or deflationary bias. The second relates to the instabilities associated with the use of a national currency as an international currency. As this was emphasized by Robert Triffin in the debates of the 1960s, it came to be called the Triffin dilemma.

The nature of this problem was significantly transformed, however, by the transition from the dollar-gold exchange standard to the fiduciary dollar standard. Since the accumulation of international reserves by developing countries basically involves foreign exchange reserves, the system forces a net transfer of resources from those countries to the major economies issuing the global reserve currencies. This third flaw of the system can therefore be called the inequity bias which as pointed out by the Zedillo Commission, created as part of the preparations for the 2002 Monterrey Conference on Financing for Development is a form of "reverse aid" (United Nations, 2001).

Furthermore, the inequities of the system have increased with the huge accumulation of foreign exchange reserves in the developing world over the past two decades as a result of the need for self-protection generated by highly pro-cyclical capital flows to developing countries and the lack of adequate "collective insurance" to manage the balance of payments crises. However, although such reserve accumulation may be a rational response of each developing country to the problems posed by the global system, it generates "fallacy of composition" effects that contribute to global imbalances, and thus to the potential instability of the system (Ocampo, 2007/08). This interaction between the second and third flaws of the system can be called the inequity-instability link. As the three flaws follow a historical sequence, it is, therefore, relevant to discuss them in terms of the historical debates on the design of the international monetary system.

The Anti-Keynesian Bias

As already noted, the first of these problems was highlighted by Keynes during the debates that surrounded the creation of the BWIs, particularly the IMF (see a fascinating account of these debates in Skidelsky, 2000: Part Two). The fundamental problem is that the current system, as indeed all international monetary systems that have preceded it, places the burden of macroeconomic adjustment on countries running balance of payments deficits. These countries have to adjust, either because they lack adequate external financing, or because they view as undesirable the associated increase of their debt ratios or, more generally, their net liability position vis-a-vis the rest of the world. Surplus countries may also face pressures to adjust, particularly those associated with the domestic inflationary effects that balance of payments surpluses generate. But the external pressures to adjust that they face are weaker or, indeed, non-existent. This asymmetric burden of adjustment, in turn, generates a global deflationary bias. This bias is particularly strong during global crises when the lack of adequate financing forces deficit countries to adjust.

Since Keynes' (1942-43) proposal to create a more symmetric system by establishing an International Clearing Union was not accepted, the Bretton Woods system was born with this inherent flaw. But even a system in which all deficit countries can automatically finance their deficits may still face a deflationary bias in so far as the macroeconomic policy authorities respond asymmetrically to the build-up of a net external liability compared to a net external asset position.

The debates surrounding the creation of the BWIs were, of course, overburdened by the expectation that the Second World War would leave the US with a structural balance of payments surplus (using the terminology Latin American structuralists later made popular) i.e., a surplus that, within reasonable bounds, cannot simply be corrected by exchange rate adjustments whereas Great Britain and Western Europe, in general, would be left with structural deficits. This made the US quite reluctant to adopt a system in which it would have to provide virtually unlimited financing to Europe. The US offered instead a very imperfect substitute, the "scarce currency clause", which has never been used. More important was the acceptance by the US of capital controls as an essential feature of post-war arrangements.

The feared structural surpluses and deficits did indeed materialize in the form of what came to be called the "dollar shortage", with the solution coming in the form of the US providing financing to Western Europe through the Marshall Plan and a regional arrangement, the European Payments Union, both of which paved the way for the eventual restoration of current account convertibility, which was more or less complete by 1958 when the European Economic Community was born. The broad-based adoption by European countries of capital account convertibility would only come much later and was only completed in 1990, soon to be followed by a set of the major European balance of payments crises.

The Triffin Dilemma

As Kregel (2009) has recently emphasized, the anti-Keynesian bias implies that the most fundamental problem of any international monetary arrangement is the operation of the adjustment mechanism in the face of global imbalances, rather than the specific asset that serves as the international currency. Nonetheless, the role of the dollar at the center of the system generated problems, which were debated in the 1960s. Robert

Triffin (1961, 1968) emphasized the essential issue: an international reserve system based on a national currency is inherently unstable. Given the importance that the Triffin dilemma has assumed in recent discussions, including its specific mention in the Chinese critique of the current system, it is worth quoting the original formulation at length:

[...] reactions of the outer countries [tend to generate] generalized waves of confidence or diffidence in the future convertibility and stability of the dollar. This makes the position of the center country highly precarious in the long run. It can, in the early phases of the popularity of its currency as a reserve instrument, finance much larger and more persistent deficits than it would be able to incur otherwise. If, however, the center country uses its leeway in this manner, the time is bound to come when other countries will shift from dollar hoarding to dollar dishoarding [...].

On the other hand, if the United States restores full balance in its external transactions, it will cease to feed a world reserve pool [...].

In either case, the use of a national currency as a primer feeder of reserve assets for the rest of the world is bound to introduce a highly erratic and unpredictable factor both in the much-vaunted mechanism of balance-of-payments adjustment and in the actual pace of growth or contraction of the world reserve pool (Triffin, 1968: pp. 87-88).

A major issue at the time, of course, was the possibility that other countries could transform their dollar reserves into gold. The attempt to collectively manage the erosion of the gold backing for the dollar through the "gold pool" ultimately proved to be futile (Eichengreen, 2007). This eventually led to the abandonment of dollar-gold convertibility in the early 1970s. The discussions of the 1960s, therefore, focused on ways to create, in a more orderly (or less "capricious", to use the preferred term at that time) manner, an adequate supply of world liquidity free from the inherent instability generated by the Triffin dilemma. Although different alternatives were suggested, the solution was the creation of a global fiduciary asset SDRs which was expected to become the main global reserve asset over time (see an account of this history in Solomon, 1977, chs 4-8).

As a digression, it should be pointed out that an interesting alternative proposed in the 1960s was to design a commodity-based reserve system (Hart, Kaldor, and Tinbergen, 1964). This idea, which goes back to Keynes' Treatise on Money, had interesting countercyclical features: world liquidity would automatically increase during global business downswings, which tended to depress commodity prices, and automatically decreased during business upswings, when commodity prices boomed. Equally interesting, this countercyclical effect would benefit developing countries, which were large producers of raw materials and thus most adversely affected by the pro-cyclical pattern of commodity prices.

The transition to the fiduciary dollar standard did not eliminate the Triffin dilemma but changed its features. The US was now able to run "much larger and more persistent deficits than it would be able to incur otherwise", without facing the constraint of dollar-gold convertibility, as flexible exchange rates would take care of adjusting the supply and demand for dollars. To the extent that the US does not regard the actual or likely weakening of its currency as a problem to be corrected, as has been typical in recent decades, this has made US monetary policy even more independent than during the era of the dollar-gold exchange standard. It has also implied that, contrary to Keynes' views, the reduced constraints on US balance of payments' deficits imply that the fiduciary dollar standard could actually generate an inflationary, rather than a deflationary bias.

The deterioration in the current account since the mid-1970s and the eventual transformation of the US investment position into a net liability position from the second half of the

1980s are both the result of the greater freedom that the US has to run balance of payments deficits and the inflationary bias that the system generates, at least during business cycle upswings. In this regard, it must be recalled that the US generally ran current account surpluses when the dollar-gold exchange standard prevailed, and dollar liquidity provision to the rest of the world was made through the capital account. The counterpart was, of course, the building of a large US investment position abroad. In contrast, under the fiduciary dollar standard that followed, the US current account deficits became the rule rather than the exception.

As Figure 1 indicates, the joint evolution of the US current account deficit and the real exchange rate of the major reserve currency have been reflected in three dominant patterns over the past three and a half decades: (1) a long-term deterioration in the current account; (2) increasingly intense cycles of both the current account and the real dollar exchange rate; and (3) although exchange rate fluctuations have played an important role in the determination of the US current account, major corrections of US deficits have been associated with US slowdowns or recessions which, in turn, had major contractionary effects on the world economy. The correction of the US deficit in 2008 and 2009 is part of the latter pattern.

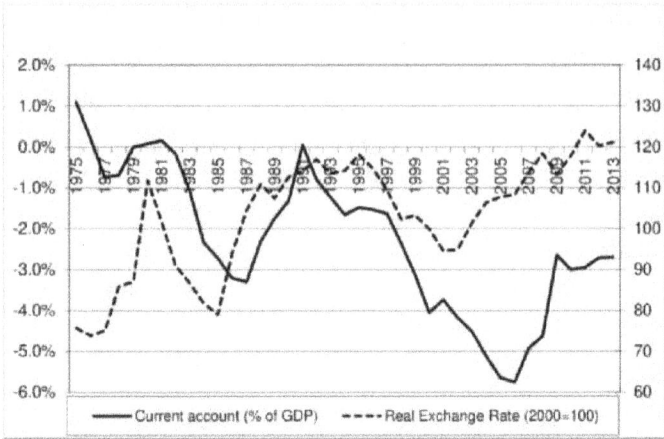

During the three and a half decades that the fiduciary dollar standard has been in place, the Triffin dilemma has displayed somewhat different characteristics from those in the past, when it was originally formulated. In short, it has shown an inflationary bias during upswings in the business cycle, particularly the most recent ones, and has generated unprecedented -- and, indeed, increasing -- volatility in both the US current account and the real dollar exchange rate. As a result, the dollar has increasingly lost what, in fact, is the essence of a good international reserve asset: a stable value. A major implication of the strong fluctuations in the US deficit is, of course, that the generation of global liquidity has become even more "erratic" or "capricious" than under the original Bretton Woods system.

It should be emphasized that the length and intensity of the most recent and longest cycle of the US current account have determinants that go beyond the US economy. In particular, although the appreciation of the dollar in the second half of the 1990s helps explain the renewed deterioration in the current account, the magnitude of this deterioration is undoubted, associated with the role of the US as the "consumer of last resort" during the major crisis in emerging markets that started in East Asia in 1997. In this context, the 2001 US recession only had minor effects on its current account. Furthermore, the deterioration of this deficit up to 2006, despite the gradual, but strong depreciation of the dollar that started in 2003, can only be explained by the fallacy of composition effects of self-protection in the developing world (see the next section).

The length and intensity of this long phase of the US current account deficit that transformed its net investment position into a net liability position another unprecedented condition of the country at the center of the global reserve system has, for many years, generated fears that official and private agents may be unwilling to continue to accumulate dollar assets (Summers, 2004; Williamson, 2004). As we will see below, the recent crisis generated some paradoxes in this regard, but the risk to the global reserve system of reduced demand for dollar assets is of renewed concern. The views expressed by the Chinese central bank governor in March 2009 are an indication that this risk will continue to be at the center of concerns regarding the sustainability of the current global reserve system.

From the point of view of the US, its position at the center of the current global reserve system has had both positive and negative implications. On the positive side, the most important advantage is that it does not face the constraint of dollar-gold convertibility, and thus enjoys greater monetary independence. The system also generates a demand for US Treasury bonds, which helps to finance the US fiscal deficits. As the US has, by now, accumulated important net liabilities with the rest of the world, another interesting advantage is that dollar depreciation generates a positive wealth (real balance) effect, as such a change increases the value of foreign assets owned by US residents, while their liabilities remain unchanged. This also implies, however, that depreciation of the US dollar has a weaker effect in correcting its current account deficit, as the wealth and relative price effects of such depreciation run in opposite directions (United Nations, 2005: ch. I). On the negative side, the fact that

US current account deficits are necessary to provide a net supply of dollar assets to the rest of the world implies that it does not entirely capture the benefits of its expansionary monetary and fiscal policies (Stiglitz, 2006: ch. 9).

Growing Inequities of the System and the Inequity- Instability Link

The transfer of resources from developing countries to the US that the system requires its inequity bias was built into its initial post-war design. However, they remained limited as long as developing countries' foreign exchange reserves were not sizable. As Figure 2 indicates, the level of these reserves was not unlike those held by industrial countries up to the 1980s about 3 percent of GDP; China had reserves equivalent to 6 percent of GDP at the end of that decade.

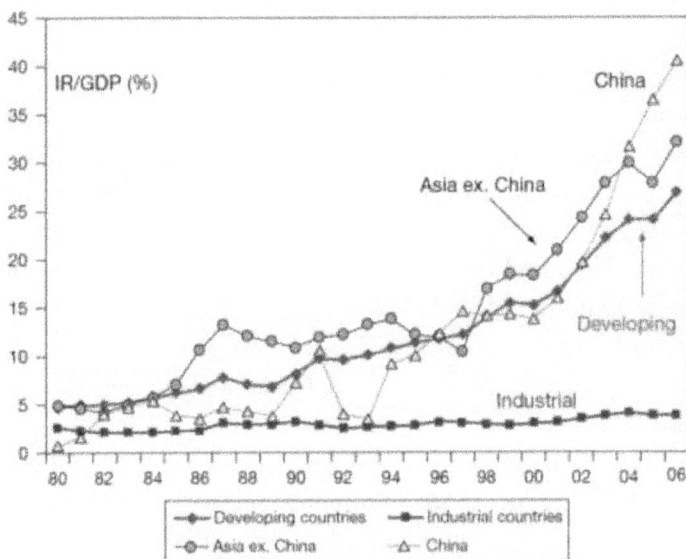

In contrast, over the past two decades, such reserves boomed and started to diverge from those of industrial countries, with China the most aggressive. By 2007, it had accumulated non-gold reserves equivalent to 46.7 percent of its GDP. The boom in reserve accumulation was equally impressive in the rest of the developing world and all regions (Table 1). By 2007, middle-income countries, excluding China, and low-income countries held foreign exchange reserves equivalent to 20.6 percent and 16.2 percent of GDP respectively. The major waves of foreign exchange reserve accumulation followed the two major financial crises experienced by the developing world the main Latin American debt crisis of the 1980s and the broad-based crisis of emerging market countries that started in East Asia in 1997. In this sense, they can be seen as a response by developing countries to the risks generated by increased openness trade opening, domestic financial liberalization, and capital account liberalization. However, although reserve accumulation started after the Latin American crisis of the 1980s, the Asian crisis was the most important turning point. It revealed, in particular, the lack of appropriate global institutions to manage emerging and developing country crises, and the particular deficiencies associated with the only form of "collective insurance" available: highly conditional IMF lending. As a result of this trend, the annual additional demand for reserves by developing countries, excluding China, shot up from US$299 billion (an average of US$43 billion per year) in 1991-97 to US$1,593 billion (US$319 billion per year) in 2003-07; the accumulation of reserves by China has been equally impressive in the recent period.

The recent pattern of reserve accumulation differs, of course, across countries and regions (see, among others, Akyuz, 2008; Carvalho, 2009; Yu, 2007). The largest group of countries continued to run current account deficits during the 2003-2007 global boom; for them, the only source of reserve accumulation was net capital flows. The second group, which includes China and several major mineral exporting countries, ran joint current account and capital account surpluses. The third is basically oil exporters with strong current account surpluses that are net exporters of capital.

There are three competing explanations for this increase in the demand for reserves by developing countries. The first, which I view as the most compelling, is that reserve accumulation is the result of "self-protection" in a broad sense which, as I will argue below, can also be seen as a countercyclical motive. This interpretation receives its most important support from the fact that the major waves of reserve accumulation have followed the two most important financial crises in the developing world.

A second explanation is provided by the "Second Bretton Woods" literature (see Dooley, Folkerts- Landau, and Garber, 2003). According to this school of thought, the basic explanation for reserve accumulation is "mercantilism", particularly by East Asian countries' undervaluation of their exchange rates as part of their export-led strategies. A reinforcing factor may be the lack of appropriate mechanisms for exchange rate coordination in export-led economies, which generates incentives to keep exchange rates competitive a point made some time ago by Sakakibara (2003) in calling for increasing macroeconomic policy coordination in East Asia. One implication of this view is that, for these countries, the benefits of stable, but weak exchange rates exceed the costs of reserve accumulation. An implication at the global level is that, for the same reason, these countries are willing to continue financing the US current account deficit.

The idea that competitive exchange rates and strong current account balances tend to accelerate economic growth in developing countries has, of course, a respectable tradition in the development literature (see, for example, Rodrik, 2007; Frenkel and Taylor, 2007; Prasad et al., 2008; Frenkel and Rapetti, 2009). However, this interpretation misses one important empirical fact: that reserve accumulation in the developing world is closely associated with fluctuations in capital flows -- i.e., that it tends to smooth out the pro-cyclical capital flows that affect developing countries (Ocampo, 2007/08, 2009). Indeed, one basic explanation provided in the literature for the strong association between a strong current account and economic growth is that it reduces dependence on volatile capital flows.

A third explanation for reserve accumulation is the "financial stability" motive (Obstfeld, Shambaugh, and Taylor, 2008). The basic argument is that international reserves are necessary for financially open economies to counter the incentives to eventually transform money balances into foreign exchange (i.e., capital flight). However, the fact that reserve fluctuations are closely associated with capital account cycles means that it is difficult to distinguish this from self-protection.

The self-protection motive can be understood in a broad sense as the attempt by developing countries to manage the strong pro-cyclical shocks they face in a globalized economy. These shocks originate in the pro-cyclical patterns of the capital flows to these countries, but also in the pro-cyclical patterns of commodity prices and the volume of international trade. In this sense, the demand for reserves is the result of the application of a broad "precautionary" principle learned from financial crises. In particular, experience indicates that allowing the real exchange rate to appreciate and the current account to deteriorate sharply during foreign exchange booms almost inevitably leads to a balance of payments crisis and is very common to both the balance of payments and domestic financial crises once the temporary condition of foreign exchange availability comes to an end. It makes sense, therefore, to respond to cyclical swings in export revenues by accumulating foreign exchange during booms to be used during subsequent crises.

In so far as cyclical shocks from the capital or trade accounts tend to generate pro-cyclical macroeconomic policy responses (Kaminsky et al., 2004; Stiglitz et al., 2006; Ocampo and Vos, 2008: ch. IV), active foreign exchange management can be seen as an attempt to increase the room for maneuver of

19

countercyclical macroeconomic policies (Ocampo, 2008; Ocampo et al., 2009: ch. 7). In this sense, the self-protection motive can be renamed "countercyclical". It is also important to emphasize that generally, the "intermediate" policy target is the exchange rate. So, smoothing out the effects of external shocks on the exchange rate is, in a sense, the essential feature of self-protection or countercyclical foreign exchange management.

Interestingly, in the case of capital account fluctuations, the self-protection motive goes beyond the Guidotti-Greenspan rule, according to which countries should keep foreign exchange reserves at least equivalent to short-term external liabilities. Indeed, to the extent that capital account fluctuations involve medium-term cycles (Ocampo et al., 2007, ch. I; Ocampo, 2008), the demand for precautionary international reserves should be proportional to total external liabilities, with the proportion larger for economies that have liberalized their capital accounts more.

Foreign exchange reserve accumulation is costly, both because foreign exchange reserves have low yields and there are costs associated with sterilizing its domestic monetary effects (Rodrik, 2006). Some alternative strategies should be considered. Saving exceptional export receipts and associated fiscal revenues from natural resource-intensive activities, have long been accepted as good practice, and are equivalent to reserve accumulation. In contrast, exchange rate flexibility to increase the room for maneuver of countercyclical monetary policy, a favorite instrument of orthodox inflation targeting, is not a good alternative, as it merely transfers the pro-cyclicality of foreign exchange availability to the exchange rate and is likely to reproduce the risks that self-protection is trying to avoid the generation of unsustainable current account deficits during booms.

In this regard, one paradox of macroeconomic policy management that characterizes developing countries in recent decades is that exchange rate flexibility has been generally complemented by active interventions in foreign exchange markets and rising demand for reserves. This has made flexible, but highly interventionist exchange rate regimes quite common in the developing world. This is not so much a reflection of "fear of floating", but rather a recognition that, as much as fixed exchange rates, clean floats generate pro-cyclical effects on the economy, albeit of a different nature (Ocampo, 2008). In this sense, and when the source is pro-cyclical capital flows, a better strategy is to regulate capital flows. In particular, to the extent that controls on inflows can reduce the magnitude of reserve accumulation, they reduce the cost of foreign exchange management. In fact, the need to accumulate reserves when capital inflows are excessive destroys the rationale for capital inflows in the first place, which is to transfer resources to the recipient country. It also undermines the other rationale for capital account liberalization to diversify risks as countries feel they need larger foreign exchange reserves to protect themselves against capital account reversals.

As already pointed out, the choice of self-protection is associated with the fact that the globalized economy we live in lacks adequate collective insurance. Furthermore, available IMF crisis lending is deemed unacceptable by many countries due to the conditionalities typically attached. In the past, these have included the adoption of pro-cyclical macroeconomic policies during crises that self-protection seeks to avoid (United Nations, 2009b). In this sense, the self-protection or countercyclical motive behind the high demand for foreign exchange reserves by developing countries is associated with both pro-cyclical capital account and trade shocks and the perception of inadequate mechanisms at the global level to provide liquidity to developing countries during balance of payments crises.

What matters, from the point of view of the global reserve system, is recognition that self-protection or countercyclical foreign exchange management while understandable from the point of view of the individual country generates fallacy of composition effects that tend to worsen global imbalances and generate a global deflationary bias. Indeed, if a large group of developing countries follows this route, they generate a current account surplus and an additional demand for "safe assets" that can be used as reserves. They will then have contractionary effects on the world economy unless matched by current account deficits and the supply of such assets by industrial countries. As indicated earlier, during the 2003-2007 global boom, both were supplied by the US, but in an unsustainable way, as the current crisis and renewed fears of loss of value of dollar-denominated assets have underscored. This is the essence of the inequity-instability link.

Therefore, self-protection is not only costly for individual countries, but also a source of global instability. However, the problem cannot be solved simply by asking developing countries to appreciate their currencies and to generate current account deficits as this has proven to be a risky combination in the past as revealed again during the current crisis by the collapse of several Central and Eastern European economies that pursued this strategy. We must start by addressing the reason for the desire for self-protection, namely the strongly pro-cyclical capital and trade flows and the inadequacy of collective insurance for the balance of payments crises in short, by reforming the global reserve system.

Reforming The System
Alternative Reform Routes

The proponents of the Second Bretton Woods hypothesis have recently argued that the current crisis was not accompanied by a run on the dollar, but rather, by its appreciation (Dooley, Folkerts-Landau and Garber, 2009). However, we should not presume that the current global monetary system is therefore stable. The strengthening of the dollar after the financial meltdown of September 2008 was the result of two factors. The first was the demand for dollars to finance withdrawals from non-banking financial institutions in the US -- an important part of the strong de-leveraging process unleashed by the crisis. The second reason was the "flight to safety" in the context of a limited supply of alternative "safe assets". In particular, the absence of a unified European bond market and the perception by many agents that the euro is backed by a heterogeneous group of countries of unequal strength has meant that the assets of only a few European countries are considered comparable with those of the US as "safe assets", but their supply has been more limited. However, with the gradual return to normalcy, downward pressures on the dollar returned in the second quarter of 2009. The yen has also strengthened due to the reversal of the Japanese "carry trade" a phenomenon similar to the demand for dollars generated by deleveraging.

An effect of the crisis with longer-term implications is the reduction of global imbalances. As during previous US recessions, the US current account deficit has been narrowing (Figure 1). With the reduction of commodity prices, the surpluses of several commodity-exporting countries were significantly eroded or even disappeared. The collapse of world trade has had similar effects on the surpluses of some major manufacturing exporters, including Japan, some other East Asian countries, and, more recently, even China. Nonetheless, although the reduction of global imbalances reduces the risks of collapse of the current reserve system, new risks have been generated by the massive expansion of the US Federal Reserve balance sheet and the large US federal fiscal deficits, which are projected to increase the US public sector debt to levels not experienced since the Second World War. Thus, the global system is certainly not free from a dollar crisis. One way the system could naturally evolve is, of course, by becoming a fully multi-currency reserve system a feature which, as has been pointed out, is already present, but remains a secondary feature of the current world monetary system. The advantage of a multireserve currency arrangement is that it would provide all but especially developing countries the benefit of diversifying their foreign exchange reserve assets. However, none of the other deficiencies of the system would be addressed. In particular, it would continue to be inequitable, as the benefits from the reserve currency status would still be captured by industrial countries (though a few developing countries, particularly China, would be able to benefit from reserve diversification by other countries). But this reform would not eliminate the deflationary or anti-Keynesian bias of the system, nor would it reduce developing countries' need for reserves for self-protection.

The exchange rate flexibility among major currencies is, paradoxically, both an advantage and a potential cost of a multicurrency system. The benefit would be derived from the absence of the major problem the two previous systems faced namely, the eventual unsustainability of fixed-rate parities. This was, indeed, a major problem that led to the collapse of both bimetallisms in the nineteenth century and the original Bretton Woods arrangement based on a fixed gold-dollar parity. However, while substitution among currencies facilitates diversification, it can lead to exchange rate volatility among the major reserve currencies. This may generate the call for fixed parities among the major currencies, which would probably be unsustainable in a world of free capital movements and would eliminate the flexibility of the system, which is precisely one of its virtues. Furthermore, all individual reserve currencies would still lack the basic advantage that a global reserve system should have a stable value. Given their high demand for foreign exchange reserves, developing countries would suffer disproportionately from the instability of reserve currencies' exchange rates.

The alternative reform route would be to design architecture based on a truly global reserve asset, which could also have broader uses in the global monetary system. Although some such voices are being heard again, returning to gold, which Keynes called the "barbarous relic", would be a non-starter. In particular, such a restoration of the role of gold would be inconsistent with the "embedded liberalism" of earlier post-war arrangements i.e., that the commitment to free markets is tempered by a broader commitment to social welfare and full employment (Eichengreen, 1996). The opposite approach would, of course, be to return to Keynes' proposal for an International Clearing Union or a similar solution (see, for example, D'Arista, 1999).

However, the most viable option is to pursue the transition launched in the 1960s with the creation of SDRs, fulfilling the objective then included in the IMF Articles of Agreement of "making the special drawing right the principal reserve asset in the international monetary system" (Article VIII, Section 7 and Article XXII). As Triffin (1968) envisioned, this would complete the transition apparent since the nineteenth century of putting fiduciary currencies (or fiat money) at the center of modern monetary systems.

This reform should certainly meet the objectives outlined by the Chinese central bank governor: "an international reserve currency should first be anchored to a stable benchmark and issued according to a clear set of rules, therefore to ensure orderly supply; second, its supply should be flexible enough to allow timely adjustment according to the changing demand; third, such adjustments should be disconnected from economic conditions and sovereign interests of any single country" (Zhou, 2009). But, in addition to providing a more orderly international monetary system rid of the Triffin dilemma, which is what these objectives imply, desirable reform should also correct, at least partially, two other problems of the system -namely, the lack of pressure on surplus countries to adjust, and the specific asymmetries that developing countries face due to pro-cyclical capital flows and the absence of adequate collective insurance.

SDR-based Global Reserve System

The nature of the expectations of SDRs that a reformed system must meet would be different today from what they were when this instrument of international monetary cooperation was created. The issue of inadequate provision of international liquidity at the centre of early post-war debates, and also surrounding early discussion of SDRs, is not important now, except in extraordinary conjunctures. If anything, the fiduciary dollar standard has actually exhibited an inflationary bias for long periods. However, this underscores the fact that the world still needs a less "erratic and unpredictable" system for providing global reserves (to use Triffin's characterization), as the call by the Chinese central bank governor for a system that ensures an "orderly supply" of the international reserve currency -- indicates. However, other problems also receiving attention in the 1960s continue to be significant or even more important today, particularly the need for a more symmetric system, access to liquidity for developing countries and associated equity issues.

The initial allocations of SDRs in 1970-72 were equivalent to 9.5 per cent of the world's non- gold reserves (Williamson, 2009). But despite the new allocation made in 1979-81, which brought accumulated allocations to SDR21.4 billion (slightly over US$33 billion at early August 2009 exchange rates), the total now accounts for an insignificant 0.5 per cent of world non-gold reserves today. The special one-time allocation approved by the IMF Board of Governors in 1997 for SDR21.4 billion, meant to equalize the benefits to new (those that joined after the previous SDR allocations) with old Fund members, will now be finally made effective, thanks to its approval by the United States Congress in June 2009. Following the call made by the G-20 in April 2009, a new allocation equivalent to US$250 billion was approved by the IMF Executive Board in July 2009. These two allocations will bring the stock of SDRs to approximately 5 per cent of global non-dollar reserves, still a very modest amount. In recent years, proposals for SDR allocations have reflected two different approaches. The first is issuing SDRs in a countercyclical way, thus avoiding issuance (or even destroying those previously made) during boom periods, when they could feed into world inflationary pressures, and concentrating them in periods of world financial stress, when they would have countercyclical effects (United Nations, 1999; Camdessus, 2000; Ocampo, 2002; Akyuz, 2005; Ffrench-Davis, 2007). The second approach proposes regular allocations of SDRs reflecting additional world demand for reserves (Stiglitz, 2006: ch. 9).

Considering the increase in reserves over the past two decades, the Stiglitz Commission's proposed allocations would be equivalent to US$150 to US$300 billion a year also the magnitude of SDRs to be issued in the long term with a countercyclical approach.

The most desirable reform involves moving to a fully SDR-based IMF with a clear countercyclical purpose. This would involve countercyclical allocations of SDRs, which would generate "unconditional" liquidity, together with countercyclical IMF financing, made entirely in SDRs, to provide "conditional" liquidity to countries facing balance of payments' crises. The best alternative to fulfill this second objective is the mechanism first proposed by Polak (1979; 2005: chs. 7-8) three decades ago -- IMF lending during crises, which would actually involve creating new SDRs (in a way similar to how lending by central banks creates domestic money, a mechanism heavily used during the current crisis), but such SDRs would be automatically destroyed once such loans are paid for. There would, of course, be limits on the magnitude of such lending, both overall and for individual countries' borrowing. The combination of these two reforms should, of course, considerably increase the size of the IMF, which has lagged significantly behind that of the world economy since the 1970s, particularly in relation to capital flows (IMF, 2009), and therefore, the provision of collective insurance.

One alternative to combining the allocations of SDRs with the lending capacity of the Fund is to treat those SDRs not used by countries to which they are allocated as deposits in (or lending to) the IMF that can be used by the institution to lend to countries in need. This would also solve the recurrent problem of making more resources available to the IMF during crises. Note, in this regard, that the traditional solution, and that approved by the G-20 in April 2009, has been to allow the IMF to borrow from member states under different modalities. But this mechanism is problematic, as it gives excessive power to the countries providing the financing (Kenen, 2001). Although it would be necessary to use it again during the current crisis, it is sub-optimal relative to quota increases, and both are, in turn, sub-optimal relative to a fully SDR-based IMF along the lines outlined above. One advantage of such a system is that it would eliminate the need for the IMF to manage a multiplicity of currencies, only a small fraction of which (30 per cent according to Polak's estimates) can be used for IMF lending.

This solution would also make clear what "backing" for SDRs involves. Strictly speaking, as with national currencies, the essential issue is not backing, but the willingness of parties to unconditionally accept fiat money when paid by another party. Backing would be provided by lending and investments made with SDR deposits. During booms, the normal instrument would be bonds from member countries that have a high level of liquidity and can be redeemed in convertible currencies. The agreed mix of such bond purchases could also be the basis of the SDR basket. During crises, of course, part of such bond holdings would be redeemed to generate funds to lend to countries facing balance of payments' crises. Both aspects would mimic the way central banks operate.

These proposals must be complemented by reforms in four other areas. First, the debate on distribution of IMF quota allocations should continue as, despite recent improvement, they do not reflect the realities of the world economy today. Of course, in a fully SDR- based IMF, "quotas" would have entirely different implications to what they have today. In particular, they would not involve actual contribution of resources to the institution, but would still determine the shares of countries in SDR allocations, their borrowing limits and, together with assigned basic votes, their voting power.

Secondly, mechanisms would have to be established to improve adjustments to the global imbalances. Increasing macroeconomic policy coordination would provide part of the solution although institutionally based in the IMF, rather than through ad-hoc arrangements (read G-7/8 or G- 20). In this regard, the multilateral surveillance of global imbalances launched by the Fund in 2006 was an interesting step in that direction, but it lacked binding commitments by the parties and an accountability mechanism. On top of that, adjustment pressures on deficits vs. surplus countries must be more symmetric to reduce the deflationary or anti-Keynesian bias. Part of the solution would be to adopt at least one part of Keynes' original plan for a post-war arrangement: the creation of generous overdraft (or in the terminology of the Fund, drawing) facilities that can be used unconditionally by all IMF members up to a certain limit and for a pre-established period. Another part would involve penalizing countries with large surpluses and/or excessive reserves, relative to the size or their economies, by suspending their right to receive SDR allocations. Of course, the definition of excessive reserves would have to take into account the exceptional demand by developing countries for reserves.

Thirdly, and crucially, from the point of view of developing countries, the solution adopted must reduce the special asymmetries that these countries face, reflected in the huge disparities in demand for reserves by developing vs. developed economies, which are at the centre of both the inequities of the current reserve system and the inequity-instability links (Ocampo, 2009). This could be done through a mix of two types of reforms: (i) asymmetric issues of SDRs, giving larger allocations to countries with the highest demand for reserves (i.e., mainly developing countries); and (ii) creation of a "development link" in SDR allocations, as proposed by the Group of Experts convened by UNCTAD in the 1960s (UNCTAD, 1965); one possible mechanism would be allowing the IMF to buy bonds from multilateral development banks with the SDRs not utilized by member states, which would then finance developing countries' demands for long¬term financial resources.

Finally, it would be essential that IMF credit lines, their conditionalities and the current stigma associated with borrowing from this institution be overcome, so that countries would actually prefer collective insurance over self-protection.9 Positive steps in this direction were taken by the IMF in March 2009 with the creation of the Flexible Credit Line for crisis prevention purposes, doubling other credit lines, and eliminating the ties between structural conditionalities and loan disbursements. One basic deficiency of the new line, however, is that it unduly divides developing countries into two categories, those with supposedly good policies and those with ostensibly bad policies, which is not only an unclear, if not arbitrary division, but also increases the risks for countries not classified in the first category, as Dervis (2008) pointed out in relation to its predecessor, the Short-term Credit Line. It also effectively transformed the IMF into a sort of credit rating agency.

Reforms could either limit the use of SDRs as a reserve asset (as it is now) or allow its broader use, as proposed in the past by Kenen (1983), Polak (2005, Part II) and, more recently, by Zhou (2009), among others. In the short-term, however, it may be useful to concentrate on reforming the global reserve system, rather than the broader monetary system. In the short term, this would imply that although the role of the dollar as the major reserve asset would be eroded, it would still keep its role as the major international means of payment, also creating demands for associated services of the US financial system (Cooper, 1987, ch. 7).

As pointed out recently by Bergsten (2007), and as envisioned in the debates of the late 1970s, it would be useful to create a substitution account, which would allow countries to transform their dollar reserves into SDR-based assets issued by the Fund, to provide stability to the current system. The June 2009 IMF decision to issue SDR-denominated bonds to some emerging economies could be considered a step in that direction. Although part of the potential costs for the IMF of such an account could be financed with its gold reserves and even by the new SDR allocations, it would be difficult, however, to adopt such mechanisms without the US assuming at least part of the associated risks a problem that blocked the adoption of this mechanism three decades ago.

The current environment could actually be a good time to introduce these reforms. First, the inflationary risks associated with SDR issues are minimal. Second, the United States would continue to enjoy full policy freedom to pursue the expansionary fiscal and monetary policies it has embarked on, without having to take into account the implications for the stability of the current reserve system. It would also free the US from the need to generate current account deficits to provide world liquidity, which has adverse aggregate demand effects for its economy. And it would continue to enjoy, in any case, the benefits of the use of the dollar as the dominant means of payment in the world.

Complementary Role of Regional Monetary Arrangements

Regional monetary arrangements should be considered part of the broader reform of the international monetary system. Indeed, as I have argued before (Ocampo, 2002), the IMF of the future should be conceived as the apex of a network of regional reserve funds that is, a system closer in design to the European Central Bank or the Federal Reserve System rather than the unique global institution it currently is. By providing complementary forms of collective insurance and fora for macroeconomic policy dialogue among regional partners, regional arrangements would help increase the stability of the global monetary system. Such arrangements would also give stronger voice and ownership to smaller countries, and are more likely to respond to their specific demands. This principle is already applied today in multilateral development financing, as the World Bank is complemented by regional development banks and, in some parts of the world, by sub-regional and inter-regional banks (Ocampo, 2006).

In the monetary arena, regional agreements can take different forms: payments agreements, swap arrangements among central banks, reserve pools, and common central banks. In the developing world, they include a few regional central banks in West Africa and the Eastern Caribbean, several regional payments agreements (e.g., among members of the Latin American Integration Association), the Latin American Reserve Fund (essentially an Andean arrangement with Costa Rica and Uruguay as well) and the 2000 Chiang Mai Initiative among the ASEAN countries, China, Korea, and Japan. The latter is, obviously, the largest of all. Although it was conceived initially as a network of bilateral swap arrangements, it has been committed since 2005 to full multilateralization, and agreed in May 2009 to complete this process, expand its resources to US$120 billion and finish the design of its surveillance mechanism. If it evolves into a structured reserve fund, this arrangement could actually issue its currency which, even if used only as an international currency, would be attractive for many central banks outside East Asia. The major criticism of these arrangements is that they are ineffective in protecting against systemic events due to likely contagion effects among its members. However, as the experience of the Latin American Reserve Fund indicates, even in a narrowly defined region, contagion does not eliminate the fact that demands for liquidity by members have different intensities and variable lags, making a reserve fund viable and desirable. This also reflects the fact that correlation among some relevant macroeconomic variables (foreign exchange reserves, terms of trade) is not necessarily very high, even if such a fund expands to include other major Latin American countries, whereas correlations in other variables (capital flows, in particular) are high, but not close to unity. Furthermore, lending at the onset of a crisis can serve as a preventive mechanism that reduces contagion, and thus, as a powerful mechanism of collective insurance. In narrower terms, reserve pooling is useful if the variability of the reserve pool is lower than that of each of the members' foreign exchange reserves (Machinea and Titelman, 2007; Ocampo and Titelman, 2009).

Regional monetary arrangements should thus be actively promoted by the international community. In this regard, a major incentive to their formation would be a provision that SDR allocations would be proportional, not only to IMF quotas but also to reserves that developing countries have placed in common reserve funds -- thus making pooled reserves equivalent to IMF quotas for this purpose (United Nations, 1999; Ocampo, 2002). They can also be the building blocks for broader reforms. The Stiglitz Commission has suggested that the new global monetary system could be built bottom-up through a series of agreements among regional arrangements (United Nations, 2009b: ch. V).

Complementary Reforms

The design of an SDR-based IMF, together with the promotion of a network of regional reserve arrangements, would go a long way to correct the basic problems of the fiduciary dollar standard under which the world monetary system has operated since the early 1990s. In principle, correcting the Triffin dilemma seems technically easier, whereas reducing the deflationary or anti-Keynesian bias and the inequities of the system vis-a-vis developing countries is harder. Any reform of the system is, in any case, politically difficult and would take time. But it is an effort worth making, as the risks that the current system faces are far from insignificant.

Obviously, the reform of the global reserve system is only part of the needed reform of the global financial architecture. Two complementary reforms have been hinted at in other parts of this paper and should be underscored in this final section.

The first is the need to place the IMF at the center of world macroeconomic policy management. This role includes strengthening the surveillance of major economies and acting as a forum for macroeconomic policy coordination. It is essential, in this regard, to overcome the traditional reliance on ad hoc mechanisms for the latter purpose - the G-5, then the G-7, and now, the G-20. This is the only inclusive way to provide a clear institutional structure for such coordination and to ensure developing countries of voice in associated processes. Indeed, the current crisis provides the opportunity to put the IMF back at the center of global macroeconomic policymaking, as its original design envisioned, and not only as a mechanism to finance emerging markets and other developing countries' balance of payments needs, the major role it has played since the mid-1970s.

The second is to rethink the positive role that capital account regulations can play in a reformed global financial system. Despite financial liberalization over the past few decades, such regulations are still allowed under the IMF's Articles of Agreement. In particular, well-designed regulations can reduce the risks that developing countries face (in a world in which finance is strongly pro-cyclical), expand the room for maneuver of countercyclical macroeconomic policies, and reduce the costs of self-protection. Such regulations could include reserve requirements on cross-border flows, minimum stay periods, and prohibitions on lending in foreign currencies to economic agents who do not have revenues in those currencies. The Fund should be encouraged, not only to tolerate but to actually advise countries on what regulations to impose in particular circumstances. Indeed, it is hard to understand why the focus on the global regulatory structure that should emerge from the crisis, particularly macro-prudential regulations, has neglected this issue, by concentrating exclusively on national prudential regulations (regional in the case of the European Union), leaving aside the risks associated with cross-border flows.

CHAPTER 2

Reforming The International Monetary System In The 1970s And 2000s: Would A Special Drawing Right Substitution Account Have Worked?

The financial crisis of 2008 demonstrated the US dollar's dominance in international finance and prompted calls to reform the international monetary system (IMS). European banks scrambled to retain dollar funding for their huge global dollar assets: a dollar shortage gripped funding markets (McGuire and von Peter 2009). To ease this shortage, the Federal Reserve extended dollar credit to major central banks, eventually without limit, and to selected emerging market central banks.

This demonstration of the dollar's pre-eminence raised again the long-standing issue of the advisability of the IMS's reliance on a single national currency. James (2009), Eichengreen (2011), and McKinnon (2012) have argued that US leadership can stabilize a dollar-centered system. Others view 'dollar hegemony' as incompatible with pluralism, which would instead entail collective (not national) control of global liquidity, fair sharing of any rents, no national privileges, and protection against the hegemon's errors or self-dealing.

At the same time, the financial crisis brought back into the spotlight a long-standing alternative global reserve asset, the Special Drawing Right (SDR). To counter a contraction in private financing, the US Treasury supported the proposal of Edwin (Ted) Truman (2009a, 2009b) for a one-time increase in the allocation of SDRs to International Monetary Fund (IMF) members in August 2009. The IMF also signed bilateral agreements to issue SDR-denominated notes, which Ocampo (2010a) interpreted as a step towards a larger transformation of dollars held in official reserves. However, the SDR 161 billion increase left SDRs still with only a single-digit percentage of global foreign exchange reserves (Ocampo 2010b, p. 331; Obstfeld 2011).

The widely-read March 2009 statement of Xiaochuan Zhou, governor of the People's Bank of China, invoked the Triffin dilemma in arguing for 'an international reserve currency that is disconnected from individual nations and can remain stable in the long run, thus removing the inherent deficiencies caused by using credit-based national currencies' (Zhou 2009). This was the generalized dilemma as stated by Padoa- Schioppa (2012): national control of global liquidity does not, in general, produce an outcome that is optimal for the world. Zhou also advocated centralization of reserves in the IMF through 'an open-ended SDR- denominated fund based on the market practice, allowing subscription and redemption in the existing reserve currencies.' The IMF showed interest (IMF 2011).

With central bank balance sheets swollen from holdings of domestic or foreign bonds, those who seek pluralism and diversification from the dollar can argue merely for further SDR issues. Instead, diversification of official foreign exchange reserves would require their transformation into holdings denominated in other currencies. Accomplishing this in an off-market transaction, so as not to depress the dollar's exchange rate, was the core idea of the substitution account.

Policymakers active in the 1970s, when the dollar was weak and global inflation high, have recently revisited this device for transforming liquid assets from the dollar to other currencies: Bergsten (2007a, 2007b), Wijnholds (2009), Boorman and Icard (2012), Camdessus (2012) and Padoa-Schioppa (2012). On the US side, participants in the late 1970s discussion about a substitution account have reconsidered the issues (Kenen 1983, 1994, 2005, 2010a, 2010b, 2010c; Bergsten 2007a, 2007b; Cooper 2009). A younger generation (e.g. Angeloni et al. 2011) has also considered a substitution account in some scenarios, but Farhi et al. (2011, p. 45) found 'no satisfactory answer' to the question of who should bear the exchange risk. This article seeks to inform the renewed interest in the substitution account by analyzing how it would have performed had it been set up along the lines of the international dialogue that ended in 1980. Kenen (2010a, 2010b) concluded from such an exercise that the account would have had to have been 'topped up' by the United States by about US$475 billion to break even from 1980 to 2008. Since he took this cost to be small relative to the US economy, he advocated such a scheme today.

We contend that he did not do justice to the issues that divided policymakers in 1980. These include the related questions of the interest rate to be paid by the US Treasury on dollars placed into the account and the means for sharing possible shortfalls arising if uncovered interest parity failed to hold. Records from the period, now located in archives, show that the IMF projected that the account could well run substantial deficits overtime for which participants would somehow have to compensate.

In what follows, we describe in Section II the evolving substitution account as proposed from 1973 to 1980. A longer perspective makes clear why it was ultimately rejected. Next, Section III profiles the key outstanding issues, again relying not only on published accounts, like Sobol (1979), Wallich (1980), Micossi and Saccomanni (1981), Gowa (1984), and Boughton (2001) but also on archival sources from the IMF, the BIS and the UK Treasury. Section IV reports simulations of the substitution account's performance depending on the resolution of major outstanding issues. Section V concludes.

II. What Was the Substitution Account?

The concept of exchanging dollar reserve assets for a reserve unit issued by the IMF or another multilateral agency had a long period of gestation towards what was ultimately a stillbirth. From the early 1960s, the sustainability of the Bretton Woods system of using national currencies as reserve assets concerned many observers. Most prominently, the Triffin dilemma predicted a loss of confidence in the US dollar's gold link as the value of official liquid claims on the United States increased. More generally, Triffin argued for the need to choose the rate of global reserve growth collectively rather than allow it to be a by-product of national decisions.

Very early on, many schemes shared the idea of a neutral unit of account issued by a multilateral fund against the deposit of officially held dollars. At first, US unwillingness to consider any scheme that would replace the dollar blocked progress, but starting in 1965, as the US balance of payments problems persisted, President Lyndon B. Johnson's administration embraced the reform discussions then underway in the Group of 10.

In the absence of US objections, the talks gained traction and culminated in a resolution that met half of the goal: the creation of a new reserve unit that IMF members would create, but not as a way to transform existing foreign exchange reserves. Rather than transforming an existing asset stock, the reform was intended to assert collective control over the flow of future reserve creation.

In setting up the SDR, ambiguity triumphed over the clarity of purpose, as officials compromised to meet expectations that had been built up for an announcement at the Rio IMF Annual Meeting in September 1967. Careful terminology avoided the label of reserve asset and the SDR was designed to add to rather than to replace existing reserves. US and UK officials referred to it publicly as front-line reserves while French officials assigned it a lesser role as a new limited form of credit (with 'reconstitution' requirements analogous to repayment after use). Ambiguous in concept and requiring a super-majority of IMF votes to make further allocations, SDR issuance remained very limited. As a result, the SDR neither contributed significantly to international official reserves nor replaced foreign exchange as the primary reserve asset. Nor did it preserve the Bretton Woods system. In 1971, the United States ceased to convert dollars into gold, and the dollar began to float against major currencies by early 1973.

The evident failure of the SDR to save the Bretton Woods system alongside wider and persistent global imbalances between the United States, on the one hand, and Japan and West Germany, on the other, led to renewed proposals for reform. The prospect of a destabilizing rush of official reserves out of the US dollar, against the backdrop of resistance by the German and Japanese authorities to the wider international use of their currencies, led the Committee of Twenty (representing the executive directors of the IMF) to consider a substitution account in 1973-1974.

The plan would allow central banks to replace a portion of their foreign exchange reserves with SDRs issued by a special account overseen by the IMF. By February 1973, the US Treasury was prepared to envisage a one-time conversion of some existing US dollar reserves into SDRs, replacing liabilities to sundry national creditors with a liability to an IMF-based substitution account. The US Treasury, however, remained wary of either undertaking a new financial obligation by guaranteeing the SDR value of the account or of paying better yields to the account than it was offering the public. If the terms were too generous, particularly considering the huge scale of possible liabilities to the account, the US Treasury (and Congress) would be unable to agree to the proposal. It thus kept an open mind on the need to transform US dollar reserves while pressing for a symmetrical global adjustment mechanism to discipline countries in persistent surplus. Others, particularly in Europe, hoped to devise a system that forced the US economy to reduce its deficits and redeem its liabilities in some form other than additional dollar liabilities. In February 1973, the IMF's US executive director, William B. Dale, dismissed the substitution account as an interesting academic exercise, noting that 'while the broad analytical issues were of great interest, the more fundamental questions lay in the obligations of debtors and creditors' and 'unless the proponents of the various schemes had some practical way of dealing with the problem of financial obligation on the part of the reserve centers [that is the United States], little progress could be made.' Certainly, without American support or at least acquiescence, no arrangement to transform US dollar reserves could go forward.

Nevertheless, the Committee of Twenty's final report in June 1974 included an illustrative proposal for a substitution account, leaving open the contested questions of interest rates payable on assets and liabilities, the disposition of any profit or loss, and the terms of liquidation. In the end, these were the very obstacles that scuppered the 1980 substitution account. Lurking behind these issues was the European desire to require the US Treasury to amortize the dollar assets in the fund over time by exchanging them for SDRs. The settlement of dollar obligations in a medium not created by the United States could make the IMS more symmetric and exert collective control over international liquidity. By the time the Committee of Twenty's report was completed, the urgency of responding to the oil crisis, inflation, floating exchange rates, development challenges, and the deficits of less-developed countries pushed the complex and longer-term topic of a substitution account down the IMF agenda. There was little political support for it and it was ignored in amendments to the Articles of Agreement agreed upon in 1976.

A depreciating dollar and negotiations for fresh allocations of SDRs revived the discussion of a substitution account at the end of 1977 (Boughton 2001, pp. 937-8; Solomon 1982, p. 285). In this context, the controversy over the potential expansionary effect of fresh allocations of SDRs on international liquidity prompted IMF Managing Director Johan Witteveen to propose in February 1978 that developed countries (including the United States) might deposit some dollars equivalent to the amount of SDRs they were allocated into a 'substitution account' to neutralize the impact on international liquidity and to increase the proportion of global reserves denominated in SDR. The IMF would invest the proceeds in long-term US Treasury securities.5 The United States was initially non-committal, although the British and Belgians supported the scheme as a way to increase the use of the SDR. After months of deliberation, the United States rejected the proposal on three grounds: it would require the US Treasury to borrow the dollars to be deposited in the account; it would be too small to make much of a difference to the distribution of global reserves and it could further weaken confidence in the dollar. The European reaction was also 'remarkably negative'. The Germans, French, and Italians rejected Witteveen's plan early on as too lenient on the Americans in terms of both the low interest they would pay on the US Treasury securities and the lack of arrangements to amortize the funds in the account (that is for the United States to pay off its liabilities). In the end, a further modest allocation of SDRs for the next three years was agreed upon and Witteveen's initiative was deferred for future study.

These early iterations of a substitution account as a vehicle to increase the role of the SDR in the IMS exposed the key obstacles that remained unresolved in 1980:

The importance of US enthusiasm to the success of any scheme, but, at the same time, the equivocal position of the US

Treasury and administration on promoting a rival to the US dollar as a reserve currency. The appropriate return on SDR assets in the account. The need for the United States to take on a major burden in any scheme. The desire of the Europeans that the United States amortize its obligations, imparting symmetry to the system.

At the beginning of November 1978, the United States reversed its benign neglect of the dollar exchange rate and took a tough set of measures that halted the dollar's decline. This change in US policy opened another opportunity to revisit the role of the dollar.

By December, the new IMF managing director, Jacques de Larosi ere, was taking soundings on a fresh and more ambitious scheme for the next Interim Committee of the IMF in March 1979. The goal was still enhancing the SDR and reducing dependence on the US dollar as a reserve currency, but the mechanism became more elaborate to overcome the objections to Witteveen's scheme and to target those countries that wanted to diversify their existing stock of reserve holdings. As reported by William Ryrie, the UK's IMF executive director, 'what was needed was a voluntary arrangement which would give countries which felt they had dollars in excess the opportunity to deposit them in exchange for some acceptable instrument and he [de Larosi ere] was thinking in terms of an SDR- denominated asset issued by the Fund.' The IMF would then invest the account's dollars in long-term US securities. US Treasury Under-Secretary Anthony Solomon was guarded when de Larosi ere approached him informally but was willing to consider the plan while de Larosi ere quietly sounded out a select group of other countries. To make a more substantial contribution to reforming the reserves system, the total amount of the account would perhaps be about US$20 billion, much greater than Witteveen's earlier proposal for about half of that amount.

Despite these preparations, the IMF executive directors in February 1979 received the proposal with caution rather than enthusiasm, although the US representative, Sam Cross, pledged to keep an 'open mind'. Cross's agnostic view was partly a ruse to avoid raising expectations. Solomon privately told his British and German counterparts that his main concern was the effect of prolonged and public discussion of such proposals on the dollar and he urged that a small, discrete group should take the discussions forward. Solomon hoped in the long term to promote the SDR as a replacement for private rather than official holdings of dollars, but he conceded that a substitution account aimed at central banks would take a step towards this goal by creating new SDR-denominated assets. German Finance Minister Manfred Lahnstein remained among the most prominent skeptics: although he 'feared too much allure for journalists in the substitution account', and also 'feared nothing would come of it', he agreed to continue deliberations in a small group. The lukewarm response of the Interim Committee in March 1979 kicked the scheme into the long grass of further investigation by the executive board. The non-committal public statement of the Interim Committee was drafted by the British by the end of February, weeks before the Committee met.

Meanwhile, ministers and deputies of the Group of Five (G5) (the United States, the United Kingdom, Japan, West Germany, and France) agreed to meet secretly to discuss the technicalities out of public earshot.

This archive-based account contradicts both Boughton's (2001, p. 938) claim that 'the most pronounced enthusiasm came from European countries itching to diversify their reserves and Robert Solomon's (1982, p. 286) contention that Antony Solo¬mon's enthusiasm added momentum. Some further insight is available from the British Treasury chair's account of the G5 working group. In June 1979, Solomon was reported to be warming to the proposal and the UK negotiator noted that 'the

US seemed prepared to go along with the creation of a substitution account' so long as the United States did not bear more than half of the exchange risk, eventual liquidation was conditional on US agreement and the SDR assets did not have a fixed maturity (that is the scheme was open-ended). Furthermore, the plan had to be presented as an enhancement of the SDR rather than as a support for the US dollar. The Germans disagreed, insisting that the purpose was to avoid a flight from the dollar to, for example, the Deutsche mark and they resisted bearing any exchange risk. The timing of the necessary legislation was also an obstacle given the need to approve the new European Monetary System. They also wanted the United States to agree to redeem some of the dollars in the account over time. The French agreed with the Germans on sharing the exchange risk and amortization and predicted resistance in the French parliament. They also argued that the success of the account would depend on a reduction of US balance of payments deficits since 'it is no good taking dollars out of the system without assurance that they won't be created all over again. The Americans clearly resisted this. The Japanese position was 'quiet'.

The British Labour government (1974-79) sought to promote international monetary reform, but Margaret Thatcher's Conservative government, elected in May 1979, had other priorities. In June 1979, Nigel Lawson (then financial secretary to the Treasury) scathingly commented, 'we should not waste valuable manpower on matters such as the IMF substitution account. Over the years I can recall no aspect of the financial scene where so much high-powered effort has been expended to so little return'. The British were not alone in their skepticism.

The Americans continued to resist bearing more than half of the exchange risk or committing to amortizing the assets. The UK representative described the 3 August executive board meeting as 'fairly fractious and did not conclude until almost midnight. He reported 'widespread feeling that a substitution account would not aid in the international adjustment process' and the recommendations from the Board to the Interim Committee remained inconclusive. The British delegation was frustrated that ministers would not receive a more definitive steer, but there was no consensus on the complex set of alternative variations of the technical aspects, particularly interest payments, burden of exchange risk and, the terms of liquidation. The IMF ministers' meeting in Belgrade in October 1979 coincided with a crisis in market confidence in the US dollar. This was not the time for a bold policy departure and differences over the technicalities remained unresolved. By April 1980, the proposal for a substitution account had been abandoned for the third time.

With respect to the 1980 iteration of the substitution account, Kenen (2010a) states that 'the proposal ... was not adopted for two reasons: the strengthening of the dollar in foreign-exchange markets at the start of the 1980s and, more importantly, the refusal of the United States to take sole responsibility for maintaining the dollar value of the SDR-denominated claims on the proposed account' (see also Widman 1982, pp. 157-8; Wilkie 2012, pp. 97-9). While the impetus for reform did recede with the dollar's recovery and the burden-sharing of risk was an important issue, this synopsis misstates the technical, political, and institutional obstacles to the scheme. It is clear that, there was no expectation that the United States would take all the exchange rate risk, although agreement over the burden-sharing remained elusive. The Europeans sought to constrain the United States to reduce its official liabilities as a price of transforming and solidifying them and, in the face of resistance, stiffened their position on yields and exchange-risk sharing. Moreover, the plan would require national legislation in many cases, which would be politically contentious and slow. Ultimately, given these uncertainties and plans for a monetary union in Europe (the European Monetary System with its

European Currency Unit was launched in March 1979), there was no political will to embark on an elaborate and possibly expensive scheme to retire a small proportion of dollar reserves.

So far, we have characterized the evolving proposal for a substitution account in political terms as a case of failed international financial diplomacy. In economic terms, the long-run solvency of the account is one of the central theorems of international finance. The open economy version of Irving Fisher's hypothesis holds that over time, currency movements offset interest differentials so that higher-yielding currencies depreciate. While this hypothesis boasts a fine pedigree, the data over the years have treated it very badly. In fact, our simulations below show that US Treasury bill yields over the last 30 years were not high enough to offset the decline of the US dollar against the SDR. Since the SDR interest rate is based on the component treasury bill rates, the substitution account in which the United States paid treasury bill rates harks back to tests of uncovered interest parity, using not short-term bank rates, but rather government bill yields (Aliber 1973).

In percent

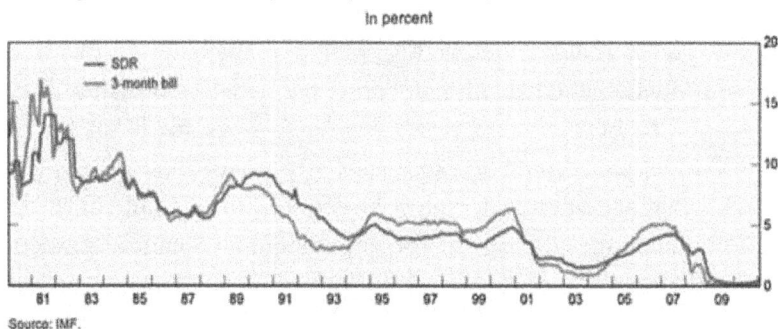

Source: IMF.

In retrospect, this test of uncovered interest parity fails. On average, Figure 1 shows that the SDR yielded 5.17% in the period from mid-1980 to the end of 2010, while the US dollar yielded slightly more at 5.37%. As we shall see, the trend depreciation of the dollar exceeded the yield cushion.

III. What Were the Major Unresolved Issues?

Any revival of the substitution account would inevitably have to deal with the unresolved issues of the 1980 negotiations. These include the interest rates on its assets and liabilities and the means to assure its solvency in the event of dollar weakness against the other currencies included in the SDR basket.

A. The Interest Rates on Account Assets and Liabilities

The substitution account would invest its dollars in non-marketable US Treasury securities, but their maturity and yields remained unresolved. Interest payable could be related to a range of US marketable securities but the British, Dutch, and others also sought to ensure that the United States paid a premium to reflect the non-marketability of these assets (and to promote the account's solvency). The interest rate and exchange rate assumptions that the Fund staff built into its simulations required an additional capital commitment amounting to 35% of the value of the account to prevent deficits from appearing. The IMF staff had a very tough assignment. From 1964-79 the US Treasury bill rate had remained below the weighted average of the SDR components even as the dollar depreciated and would have needed to be, on average, 3% higher to have made up for the dollar depreciation. The Fund staff attributed this to the special circumstance of initially high confidence in the stability of the US dollar and one-off 'lags in the adjustment of financial markets. For their simulations, IMF staff allowed the US Treasury bill rate premium over the SDR rate to fall a more modest 0.5%, 1%, or at most 1.5% short of compensating for a US dollar depreciation of 1% per annum against the other SDR currencies over the next 30 years. They also factored in some cyclical and random disturbances. These simulations clearly highlighted the importance of interest rates payable on assets and liabilities of the account to the costs of sustaining it. Higher interest rates payable by the US Treasury would reduce the commitment of extra capital by members or of IMF resources such as gold. (The interest payable on SDR- denominated assets issued by the account was less discussed; see in McCauley and Schenk 2014).

B. How to Meet Any Shortfall of Dollar Returns below SDR Returns

Technical differences in the proposals to maintain the account's solvency arose from domestic political constraints on participants and differences in the desired international adjustment process. The IMF staff simulations highlighted how, if the US dollar were to depreciate against the SDR beyond the cushion afforded by higher US interest rates, the financial balance of the account would quickly deteriorate. The viability of the account, therefore, depended on the United States following economic policies conducive to a strong dollar. Thus, in January 1980, Robert J. Whitelaw (Australia) noted, 'Ultimately, the substitution account could be effectively guaranteed only if the US Government followed economic policies that tended to maintain the value of the dollar'. Europeans worried that, with a substantial share of its dollar liabilities immobilized in the account, the United States might actually feel less pressure to adjust its balance of payments. Could the US Treasury be induced to promise to maintain the dollar's SDR value to sustain the solvency of the account? In Cooper's (2009, p. 4) phrase, this 'would be a show-stopper for the United States, since no Congress would provide an unconditional guarantee of value for assets'. If the US Treasury had to bear all the risk, it might as well, as suggested by Governor Wallich of the Federal Reserve Board, issue SDR-denominated liabilities itself rather than going through the complexities of a substitution account (Solomon 1982, p. 289). If the United States was unwilling, would the claimants on the substitution account be prepared to bear the risk to stabilize the IMS? If so, unless the account solved a prisoners' dilemma among dollar holders, they might as well continue to hold the dollars themselves and save the bother of the account. Somehow the risk had to be shared and the United States took a firm position that other participants would have to shoulder at least half of the burden of exchange risk.

One politically expedient way would be to use the IMF's resources, which in effect would implicitly share any losses among the participants. Would Europeans and less developed countries agree that IMF gold should be used to maintain the dollar's SDR value? To some Europeans, gold backing would allow the United States a free hand to adopt policies that would weaken the dollar. For less developed countries, using the IMF's gold to prop up an account that would benefit mainly rich participating countries (that is those with large dollar reserves) would contradict the agreement reached in 1976 to use the IMF's gold to create a trust fund for the poorest members. For these reasons, many of the parties involved were convinced that to ensure equity and discipline on US policy, the United States had to bear part of the burden of any losses in the account.

B.1. Sharing Rules

The distribution of any burden among depositors, the United States, and the IMF was highly contentious. As noted, the IMF staff simulation of the account's performance over 30 years allowed the dollar's downward trend to continue and examined the consequences of the interest rate differentials in favor of the dollar not affording a sufficient offset. Most discussions focused on the flow problem and members sought a solution whereby the United States would bear at least half of the shortfall of interest income from the account's dollar assets in relation to the required interest payment on SDR liabilities. The rest of the burden could be borne by depositors themselves or by IMF resources. However, Europeans worried that, if the United States bore no share of potential losses, US policy-making could face perverse incentives (that is moral hazard). At the time of the discussions, the US dollar was weakening, which suggested that there might be substantial losses to be met.

One set of solutions required all participants (including the United States) to commit to contributing a maximum amount of 'callable capital', although the distribution of burden between the United States and others was never agreed upon. One approach would first exhaust gold profits, then have a vote on whether to liquidate the account immediately; only if the decision were against liquidation would further capital be called (see McCauley and Schenk 2014 on liquidation). The burden on participants during the account's lifetime depended on the commitment of the IMF's gold to ensure the account's solvency.

B.2. Profits On Gold Sales

The amount of gold needed to support the account depended on the price of gold and the dollar exchange rate, as well as interest rate differentials. As the plan was being discussed, the rise in the dollar price of gold had outpaced the decline in the US dollar's SDR value, so that only a proportion of the account's value in gold would be necessary to ensure against any shortfall. Early simulations by IMF staff at the end of 1979 suggested that one-third of the Fund's remaining gold supply (about 32 million ounces) would be required for an account of SDR 50 billion. The value of this gold would amount to about 20% of a substitution account of such size. From 1976 the IMF had agreed to sell about one-third of its gold (then 50 million ounces) to reduce the role of gold in the IMS as newly agreed to under Article V. To this end, half was sold at market prices, and the profits were vested in a trust fund for developing economies and the other half was sold back to members at a low, historic price. With this precedent, any further sale of IMF gold was highly contentious, and also required an 85% majority vote. By April 1980, the IMF staff estimated that only 20-25 million ounces of gold would need to be committed to an account of SDR 50 billion. This new estimate brought the commitment of gold into line with the volume of gold that had recently been sold to the benefit of the developing countries.

Many members strongly resisted using the IMF's gold resources for the substitution account, since the benefits would not be distributed equitably. Joaq uin Muns (Spain) and Lamberto Dini (Italy) stressed that this was a potentially illegal use of the Fund's gold. As influential Brazilian Director Alexandre Kafka put it, 'the Fund's gold was in the last analysis owned by individual countries but would be used only to help the participants in the substitution account', mainly richer nations. Muns and Jacques de Groote (Belgium) also expressed concern that an account with 'gold backing' might resurrect the role of gold in the IMS, which had just been abandoned. Conversely, Cross (United States) and Gerhard Laske (West Germany) favored transferring gold to the account, or even immediately selling it to provide liquid and interest-earning assets and to lock in the high gold price. Cross stressed that all countries would benefit from a stronger IMS so the equitable treatment constraint did not arise, but C. D. Deshmukh (India) and Jahangir Amuzegar (Iran) expressed skepticism. At the Executive Board seminar on the subject in early January 1980, those executive directors rejecting the use of IMF gold or expressing severe reservations accounted for almost 30% of the votes in the IMF, which did not bode well for reaching 85% approval. Without the IMF's gold as a backstop, participants would find it difficult to agree on burden-sharing among themselves that could be sold to their national parliaments.

IV. Simulations of the Substitution Account Performance

Our baseline scenario finds that the substitution account would have faced recurrent difficulty. We then find that the flow issue of a higher interest rate payable by the US Treasury would have kept the account solvent while the stock issue of 25 million ounces of gold would not have.

We assume reinvestment of interest earnings so that both assets and liabilities rise with total returns, including both cumulative interest and currency valuation changes. Exchange rate revaluations are limited to the asset side since the simulations are reported in SDR terms.

Our baseline simulation assumes that the account amounted to the proposed SDR 50 billion, began at the dollar's trough in mid-1980, and benefited from the profit on 25 million ounces of IMF gold. With hindsight, even this favorable combination was a recipe for trouble. Our simulation differs from that of Kenen by sticking more closely to the original proposal whereby IMF gold rather than annual US 'topping up' would keep the account in balance.

Liabilities in SDR would have grown steadily but assets would not have, leaving an unsteady balance between them (Figure 2; see also Table 1 in McCauley and Schenk 2014). The SDR 50 billion liability would have reached an SDR 262 billion liability by 2010. Compounded at Treasury bill yields, dollar assets equivalent to SDR 227 billion would have fallen short of liabilities by SDR 35 billion or 14%. This turned out better than the IMF's 1980 projections, which suggested a 20% shortfall after 30 years with interest accrued at the Treasury bill rate. Importantly for the prospects of a sustainable account, deficits recurred. In particular, the account would have needed the support of gold as early as the Plaza Accord era in 1987, throughout the 1990s, and again for the years after the dollar's peak in early 2002.

In billions of SDRs

As a percentage of assets

Sources: IMF; authors' estimates

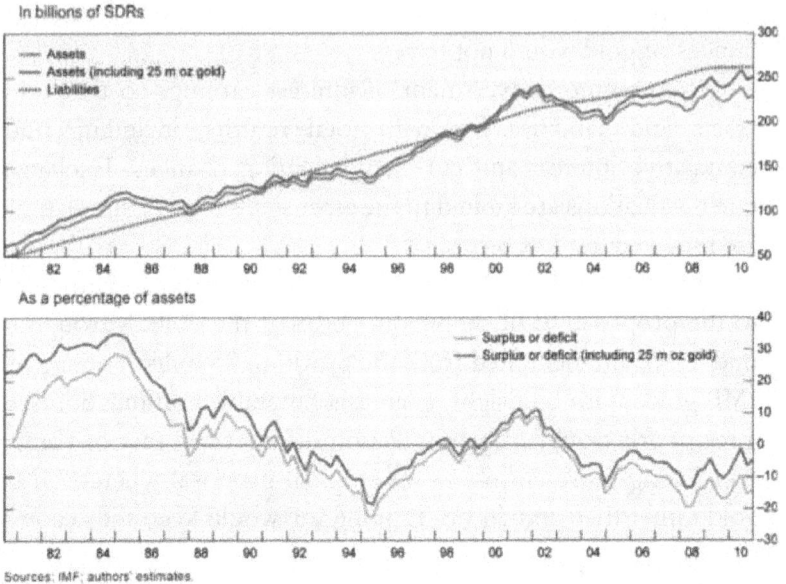

Gold profits would only have made a difference for a while. Profits on 25 million ounces of gold of as much as SDR 20 billion would have filled the gap between assets and liabilities in the late 1980s and late 1990s. However, they would have left a gap in most of the 1990s and since 2002. Thus, liquidation discussions in the 1990s could have required calling up contributions from participants. Remarkably, even near its peak price in 2011, gold profits in 2010 would not have restored balance.

While the amount of gold discussed would not have maintained solvency, higher bond yields payable by the US Treasury on the account's US dollar assets would have. In principle, compounding using a bond yield adds a term premium, which proved generous in a period of declining trend inflation. Figure 3 shows that receiving interest at the 20-year bond rate, as suggested by some protagonists at the time, the account would have racked up a considerable surplus. A fortiori, the investment in fixed-rate Treasury bonds in 1980 or 1981, then carrying

54

double-digit yields, as proposed by US Executive Director Cross, would have done wonders.

This finding helps put in a new perspective the shift by reserve managers towards longer-maturity US bonds since 1980 (McCauley and Rigaudy 2011). Without acting collectively through a substitution account, reserve managers have over the period 1980-2010 shifted from investing dollars in short-term instruments to medium and even long-term bonds. By receiving medium or long-term yields on their US dollar holdings, they have been better able to offset the effect of the decline of the US dollar's exchange rate on their reserves' total returns.

A substitution account to absorb unwanted US dollar reserves and to increase the role of the SDR has attracted IMS reformers for over a generation. In the 1970s, part of the appeal of such schemes was to develop a mechanism that might ultimately require the United States to redeem its liabilities in SDR, or at the very least would create an SDR-denominated reserve asset that could rival the dollar. Repeated efforts to design such an institution have stumbled over technical and political obstacles. Kenen (2010a) points to the refusal of the United States to bear the sole burden of losses as a key reason why the substitution account was not adopted, but negotiators did not insist that the US exclusively bear the account's risk. Nevertheless, several obstacles proved insurmountable, including the use of gold reserves, the returns on the liabilities and assets of the account, and the responsibility of the United States ultimately to redeem its outstanding US dollar liabilities. Even if these issues had been resolved, and the IMF's gold had been committed to the account, it would not have broken even with US Treasury bill returns. Oddly, an agreement might well have been reached to have the US Treasury pay the account a bond yield.

To have shrunk the share of dollar reserves substantially, the substitution account needed to become a conversion process rather than a one-shot deal. As conceived in 1980, the substitution account would have immobilized a substantial fraction of global reserves. In mid-1980, SDR 50 billion represented about 16% of global foreign exchange reserves outside of those held by the United States and a third of US dollar reserves. Our baseline scenario shows the initial SDR 50 billion growing fivefold. Yet at end-2010, this sum would have fallen to less than 5% of global reserves. Thus, although the substitution account was aimed at resolving the 'stock' problem of large existing balances of US dollar reserves, its benefit measured in stock terms would have eroded steadily over time. Thus, the substitution account would have had to have been re-opened repeatedly to solve the presumed problem. Only in this sense of an 'endogenous' process starting with an 'exogenous' 1980 deal can it be said that if 'the Substitution Account been implemented, we would have avoided the large overhang of dollar reserves that now threatens the durability of the international dollar standard' (Alessandrini and Fratianni 2009, p. 59).

A substitution account that offers a perpetually open exit from US dollar reserves addresses not a 'stock' but a 'flow' problem. This may have been (and be) what the proposers were (and are) really after—a way to turn the SDR into a more important reserve asset. Indeed, in the 1980 proposal, there was a provision to re-open the account once it had reached SDR 50 billion. However, it is hard to imagine the account being upsized unless it was at least in balance. As we have seen, this would have been rare in the case of the US Treasury paying interest at its bill rate. Moreover, additional 'deposits' would have to have been well-timed near US dollar troughs to maintain the account's performance. As is well known, tests of uncovered interest parity depend on their results on the sample period chosen. However, with the dollar near a cyclic bottom in 1980, the sample period examined was a fair test; many starting points would have produced worse results for the account.

The upshot is that proposals for a substitution account must deal with an inconvenient fact the account would not have added up even with a substantial endowment of gold profits and a favorable start date unless the United States had committed to pay a bond yield on the account's assets. Over a generation, reserve managers found their way to this result: without coordination, they extended the maturity of their dollar portfolios (in perhaps Pavlovian fashion) as dollar bond yields fell from double-digit levels. Indeed, given the current preference of reserve managers for bonds, any renewed negotiations for a substitution account would almost surely focus on the US Treasury paying bond yields. How such negotiations would proceed, and what results might be obtained over time, with the Federal Reserve having made large-scale bond purchases, and bond yields have reached very low levels, are interesting questions. Choosing the right moment to open such an account and anticipating the possible rhythm of deficits as well as surpluses on its balance sheet would pose significant challenges.

Can Special Drawing Rights Be Recycled To Where They Are Needed At No Budgetary Cost?

There is a clear rationale for recycling SDRs to countries in greater need. The shares of low-income countries (LICs) and many middle-income economies in the SDR allocation expected later this year will fall short of what they need to respond to the pandemic and its aftermath, while many advanced countries are likely to have "surplus" SDRs. And it is tempting to see this as an easy task. If the surplus SDRs issued to advanced countries is a costless windfall, surely it should not be a difficult decision, in economic or political terms, to use them for the benefit of other countries at a time of crisis?

If only it were so simple to recycle SDRs. Even if there is a strong political impetus, the combination of the necessary accounting for SDR allocations and the institutional framework in recipient countries poses significant challenges to recycling. These factors are likely to result in priority being given to a reallocation via SDR loans to the IMF's Poverty Reduction and Growth Trust (PRGT). This has so far been the main (or even the only) vehicle for the limited reuse of SDR that has occurred since the last allocation. It provides additional support to LICs and has the advantage for lenders of protecting the reserve asset qualities of their SDRs and carrying no budgetary cost. At the other extreme, donations of SDRs may be much harder to engineer.

The Obstacles

First, there is accounting. Creating new SDRs results in both a liability and an asset. The allocation is recorded by the recipient country as a liability because of the possibility that some of the allocations could be canceled although this has never happened and because interest is payable on the full value of the allocation at the SDR interest rate. On the asset side, SDR holdings rise in tandem with the allocation and earn the SDR interest rate. As long as holdings are kept in line with the allocation, the SDR is indeed a costless asset.

This Accounting Treatment Has Two Implications:

First, if SDRs are lent or donated by a country, its holdings of SDRs decline so that a net SDR interest cost is due. If SDRs are lent, this cost is offset as long as the loan earns at least the SDR interest rate. If SDRs are donated, the donor can offset the SDR interest cost by exchanging some of its other reserve assets for SDRs to restore the balance between its SDR holdings and its allocation. But this will entail interest foregone on the reserve assets exchanged for SDRs.

Second, a donation of SDRs would result in an imbalance, with liabilities exceeding assets.[3] And if restoring this balance entails an additional budgetary cost, why not simply finance a donation through the budget and not link this to the SDR allocation? Alternatively, and subject to the particular institutions, laws, and regulations of the prospective donor country, is there some means by which the SDRs can be donated without incurring a budgetary cost?

The institutional framework for SDRs and their use varies across countries. A key consideration is whether the SDR allocations are made to the central bank and then reside on its balance sheet or to another branch of government such as the ministry of finance or treasury. But, beyond that general distinction, much depends on the precise arrangements in each country.

The UK provides a good illustration of the interplay between the accounting for the SDR allocation and the institutional setup. The Exchange Equalization Account (EEA), which is controlled by the Treasury, holds the UK's reserves of gold, foreign currency assets, and SDRs.[4] This institutional setup differs from most countries in which official reserves including SDRs are on the balance sheet of the central bank.[5] But as well as highlighting the advantages of lending SDRs and the difficulty of donating SDRs, this example also shows how it may be possible to use SDR to support a donation with no net impact on the government's borrowing requirements.

The UK Example

The UK has, for several years, lent some of its SDR holdings to the PRGT. This lending reduces the UK's SDR holdings so that earnings on its holdings fall short of interest due to its allocation. But this shortcoming is offset by interest earned at the SDR interest rate on loans to the PRGT. And although lending to the PRGT has a maximum maturity of 10 years, the UK's claims remain liquid. The lending is in the form of notes which can be traded with other official entities, and the liquidity of these claims is also supported by the "encashment" regime available to lenders to the PRGT.

This allows participating lenders to seek early repayment of their loans in case of balance of payments need while also authorizing their own loans to be drawn upon to meet early repayments by other lenders. These features, coupled with the relatively low risk of lending through the PRGT, allow the EEA to treat its loans to the PRGT as fully liquid international reserves while earning the same interest as SDR holdings. In May 2020, the UK's lending agreement was amended to raise the total available to the PRGT to SDR 4 billion. Although this was one of the larger bilateral lending agreements supporting the PRGT, it approximates to only about 40 percent of the UK's existing SDR allocation.

The proposed SDR allocation would add about 14 percent to the assets of the EEA.[6] The UK's share of a $650 billion allocation would be $27.6 billion, or about £20 billion, and bring a nearly three-fold increase in the UK's SDR holdings. The increase in reserves would also be significant in relation to the recent funding of the EEA. Following the global financial crisis in 2008, official reserves were augmented "to ensure that the level of foreign currency reserves held is sufficient for the UK to remain resilient to possible future shocks." The EEA's annual report notes that "a further £6 billion in additional financing was provided in 2019-20 ... concluding the program of additional financing which has seen an additional £72 billion invested over 12 years."

Some of the resulting excess reserves from the UK's new allocation could be used to provide larger loans to the PRGT. This would have the advantages noted above for both LICs and the UK. But on a global scale, there may well be many more SDRs available from potential lenders than the PRGT could absorb. This has many dimensions. The scale of lending may become too large in relation to the PRGT reserve account which can be drawn upon to repay lenders in the event of delayed repayments by countries borrowing from the PRGT. The weakening of this important risk mitigant would become more of a concern if sharply higher lending by the PRGT brought greater risks of debt distress among LICs. In addition, while the PRGT has adequate subsidy resources to maintain commitments at the high level of over SDR 6 billion seen in 2020 for the next 3-4 years, these resources will need to be replenished at some point. Other avenues will be needed to ensure that surplus SDRs are used effectively.

A direct donation of SDRs from the UK's EEA does not appear to be possible. The current rules governing the EEA's operations, including the act under which it was established, do not suggest that there is scope for the Treasury to approve a donation from the EEA. Moreover, the EEA is closely linked to the National Loans Fund (NLF), which provides the bulk of its resources.

But there may be an indirect channel to mobilize surplus reserves from the SDR allocation for a donation. The Treasury is authorized to pay into the NLF assets of the EEA that are determined by the Treasury to be more than the amount this is required for the EEA. On this basis, the Treasury could decide to return to the NLF at least part of the "excess" reserves arising from the SDR allocation. The SDRs would remain in the EEA and be available to be exchanged for reserve currencies as needed. Some of the EEA's non-SDR reserves would be paid to the NLF; the counterpart of this decline in gross reserves would be a reduction in the EEA's liabilities to the NLF. The repayment to the NLF would entail a corresponding decline in government debt. Thus, it may be possible for the UK government to make a donation equivalent to at least part of the SDR allocation without this adding to total government borrowing prior to the SDR allocation. At the same time, the reserves of the EEA would be at least as large as they were before the SDR allocation. The donation would also not entail an interest cost. SDR holdings would not fall below the allocation, so no net SDR interest would be due. The EEA would forgo earnings on reserves paid into the NLF, but this would be offset by lower debt payments.

Budgetary approval for a donation using this channel could be considered to lie outside usual constraints. If the UK were to donate to support LICs—either directly or through special-purpose health or climate fund— this would likely require budgetary approval. But this external donation would in a real sense be costless. The donation would not have taken place without the SDR allocation, it would not add to government debt, and it would not affect domestic demand. Thus, there would be a strong case for this spending to be added to the existing budget. In particular, it should add to the aid budget. This would require a decision not to score the donation—which could potentially be large—against the current ceiling in official development assistance. To do otherwise would simply be to mobilize the unused SDRs to finance existing expenditure with no net benefit to LICs or middle-income countries in need. The UK example may not be directly applicable in facilitating donations from other countries. Every country will have its institutional arrangements, which will place different constraints on their ability or willingness to unlock SDRs to benefit LICs or middle-income countries.

But, from this UK example, a few points stand out:

Lending to the PRGT ticks all the boxes for the lender. Credit and liquidity risks are mitigated, allowing the SDRs lent to retain their reserve asset qualities and there is no interest cost. But other worthy uses may not meet all these criteria, so lenders might need to sacrifice liquidity and accept some credit risk.

In the UK case, the SDR allocation would facilitate a donation, but without the SDRs themselves being donated. This may be a useful approach in other countries considering donations. And when countries consider lending SDRs, it may be easier to lend other reserves which are excess to requirements as a result of the SDR allocation.

Even if a donation can make at no cost—as appears to be the case in the UK—this may well require a decision that goes beyond the scope of a central bank's independent mandate. If the SDRs are under the control of the central bank, it may first be necessary to transfer this control to the government.

Most importantly, the UK example suggests that a lot of work will need to be done, country-by-country, to ensure that the world benefits to the fullest from the SDR allocation.

Why Are Special Drawing Rights (SDR's) Required?

In the recent past, there have been rumors that countries like China and Russia are urging the International Monetary Fund to move away from the United States dollar-based system. These rumors suggest that these countries propose that Special Drawing Rights (SDRs) become the de facto reserve currency of the world.

One possible reason could be the fact that countries like China are fully aware of the fragile economic condition on which the United States economy stands. Also, China is forced to buy more and more United States treasury debt if it wants to keep its own economy afloat.

Hence, if a Special Drawing Rights (SDRs) based system was implemented, China and many other countries could exchange the excess dollars that they have with a basket of currencies. True, they would still end up with 44% dollars again! However, that would still be a better scenario than being 100% dependent on the United States economy as being a store of value.

Benefits of the Special Drawing Rights (SDRs) System Whether a Special Drawing Rights (SDRs) based system will replace the current dollar-based system is yet to be known.

However, there are some benefits if such a system does get implemented. The benefits are as follows:

Reduced United States Dependence: First and foremost, the entire world will no longer have to depend on the currency of the United States to trade with each other. This would eliminate what the French have nicknamed as "exorbitant privilege" given to the United States government wherein they have been placed at the center of the financial universe.

More Stable System: Since essential commodities such as gold, oil, and food grains will no longer be exclusively traded in dollars, the United States government will not be able to exert an undue influence on their prices by increasing and decreasing the money supply of dollars. A weighted average of multiple currencies would make the system more stable.

Balance of Payment Issues: If the world were to go off a dollar-based system it would resolve a lot of balance of payment issues that are being faced. The United States is running a perpetual trade deficit with countries like China. They can sustain such a budget deficit because the world depends on the dollar for its day-to-day functioning. However, if the world goes off the dollar standard, the United States would lose this privilege.

Disadvantages Of The Special Drawing Rights (SDR's) System

The implementation of Special Drawing Rights (SDRs) in place of a dollar-based system will also lead to certain issues. Some of them have been mentioned below:

Money Supply Becomes An Administrative Decision: If Special Drawing Rights (SDRs) become the reserve currency of the world, then the IMF would be in charge of regulating the money supply. Given the fact that Special Drawing Rights (SDRs) would not have an open market of their own, the decision regarding whether the money supply should be expanded or contracted would end up becoming an administrative decision.

The fact that all other economic parameters are extremely sensitive to changes in money supply, is a dangerous situation to be in.

Abstract Nature: The Special Drawing Rights (SDRs) are an abstract weighted average. They are not actual currency that can be used by people. As such, Special Drawing Rights (SDRs) will be extremely difficult to implement and manage, if they are ever introduced at the microeconomic level.

No Gold Backing: Lastly, only backing by a tangible commodity like gold makes a currency stable. Hence, replacing dollars with Special Drawing Rights (SDRs) would be like replacing one unstable system with another slightly less unstable system.

Here Are Five Key Principles For Effective SDR Reallocation.

1. Prioritize the global fight against COVID-19.

A portion of SDRs must go toward purchasing COVID- 19 tests, treatments, and vaccines by closing the ACT- Accelerator's funding gap, which is estimated to be $18.5 billion. These allocations can also be used to provide additional funding needed to achieve extensive global immunization and prevent the next pandemic.

2. Support an inclusive and green recovery.

Countries should prioritize initiatives that contribute to an inclusive and green economic recovery. These include targeting assistance to social priorities, such as education, health, social protection, job creation, and green climate investments.

3. Distribute SDR holdings in an efficient and timely manner.

While there are many innovative proposals for new funding mechanisms to reallocate SDRs, Global Citizen urges the IMF and donor countries to prioritize mechanisms that allow for money to reach countries quickly. This will ensure that the countries that need the most support to end the pandemic for their populations can access financial reserves immediately. New mechanisms, which could take up to a year to operationalize, will only delay support to low- and lower-middle-income countries that need resources now. Mechanisms such as the Poverty Reduction and Growth Trust (PRGT) and the Catastrophe Containment and Relief Trust (CCRT) are two existing options for ensuring timely, targeted support.

4. Ensure that SDR on-lending mechanisms are concessional and in addition to existing aid commitments.

The financial support offered through new SDRs should be as debt-free and concessional as possible to provide the best means of support for struggling poor countries without adding to their debt burden. Similarly, donated SDRs must be new, additional aid and not a substitute for foreign aid that wealthy countries were already planning to give.

5. Include lower-middle-income countries when considering SDR reallocations.

The World Bank estimates that the global pandemic will push 150 million more people into extreme poverty around the world, with 82% of those people in lower-middle-income countries. Despite this, these nations have largely been left out of economic support and debt relief efforts to date.

Including lower-middle-income countries, in addition to low-income countries, in any new SDR mechanism will be critical for targeting support to the countries with the highest extreme poverty rates.

While every country has been affected by the pandemic, researchers say that the global economy will suffer if COVID-19 resources and vaccines are not distributed equitably. The IMF's decision to initiate a new wave of SDR allocations will help struggling nations access COVID-19 resources and jumpstart economic initiatives to lift themselves out of poverty. World leaders can ensure that nations struggling the most can access lifesaving resources by donating a portion of their SDR holdings. By targeting their support, these initiatives can end the pandemic for everyone, everywhere, and benefit the future of low- and lower-middle-income countries.

CHAPTER 3

Special Drawing Rights: Saving The Global Economy And Bolstering Recovery In Pandemic Times

In the wake of the liquidity and fiscal crisis across developing countries generated by the global pandemic, the role of Special Drawing Rights (SDRs) has formed an important part of the discussion on economic recovery. During the crisis, developed countries have accounted for nearly 80 percent of all fiscal efforts, while many low-income countries (LICs) have cut spending or have directed more funds to repay creditors than they have to their health sectors.

In the 15 months since the start of the pandemic in March 2020, multilateral efforts have not sufficiently accelerated comprehensive efforts to respond to the multiple dimensions of health and economic crises in developing countries, particularly through financing and provision of immediate liquidity. The unequal distribution of vaccines and the emergence of new variants of the coronavirus threaten to prolong the crisis, with developing countries continuing to bear the brunt of the exacerbation of poverty and inequality. Progress towards the Sustainable Development Goals (SDGs) by 2030 has effectively been derailed, with many developing countries set back by years or decades when it comes to achieving the Goals.

In this context, there has been ample discussion of the possible role of SDRs - an international reserve asset issued by the International Monetary Fund (IMF) - when it comes to responding to the crisis. It now appears that later this year, the

IMF will allocate countries with SDRs worth a combined total of US\$ 650 billion. However, there remains much debate about precisely how SDRs can support the pandemic response and recovery, how SDRs can be directed to those countries most in need, and what kind of institutions could be set up to draw on SDRs in the pandemic response.

With these questions in mind, a group of 16 civil society organizations organized a webinar titled SDRs: Saving the global economy and bolstering recovery in pandemic times on 21 May 2021.

Opening remarks were made by His Eminence Cardinal K.A. Peter Turkson, Prefect of the Vatican's Dicastery for Promoting Integral Human Development. Speakers included:

- Vera Songwe, Executive Secretary of the UN Economic Commission for Africa
- Jose Antonio Ocampo, former Finance Minister and Central Bank Board Member of Colombia
- Daouda Sembene, Distinguished Non-Resident Fellow, Center for Global Development, and former IMF Executive Director for a group of African Countries
- Ana Corbacho, Assistant Director of Strategy, Policy and Review Department, IMF
- Esteban Perez Caldentey, Chief, Financing for Development Unit, Economic Commission for Latin America and the Caribbean (ECLAC), and
- Jayati Ghosh, Professor of Economics, University of Massachusetts Amherst.

The Purpose Of SDRs

Global reserve funds in the form of SDRs are a vital tool to provide swift and unconditional support to the global pandemic response without increasing debt. Civil society organizations and experts have called for a new allocation of US\$ 3 trillion in SDRs. Earlier this year, the IMF membership conveyed broad support for an allocation of US$ 650 billion in SDRs. They will consider a formal proposal in June, while the issuance will likely occur in August. Of this amount, low-income countries would receive US$ 21 billion - crucial relief, but not close to the US$ 450 billion in financing needs identified by the IMF to step up the pandemic response and accelerate growth. Developing countries would receive US$ 230 billion - far short of IMF estimates that last year placed emerging economies' financing needs at US$ 2.5 trillion.

During the event, Ocampo said that the most positive aspect of SDRs is that they are essentially foreign exchange reserves for developing countries, providing them with international liquidity. In light of the very limited international cooperation on debt and liquidity that has taken place, SDRs are constructive for pandemic response and recovery in developing countries. Corbacho of the IMF clarified that SDRs will boost international reserves and that this is of vital importance as an insurance mechanism in times of crisis. Expanding reserve assets also strengthens global financial resilience and confidence by sending a powerful signal of macroeconomic stability.

Corbacho went on to outline the immediate uses of SDRs in developing countries, which include building up reserve buffers, providing financial backstops, and freeing up financial liquidity for the urgent balance of payment needs. The creation of additional liquidity can occur either by the addition of SDRs to reserves freeing up other foreign currency reserves or by countries converting their SDRs to hard currency. When countries convert their SDRs to currency, they are required to pay an interest rate to the IMF. Given that the normative interest rate is at a record low of 0.05 percent, using SDRs is currently very affordable. If - or rather, when - rich countries start to normalize and unwind their expansionary policies, interest rates may rise, which countries should bear in mind.

Sembene said that, if they are well-calibrated and timely, SDRs can provide useful liquidity, but that historically SDRs have not played this role. Mechanisms to recycle and transfer SDRs must be designed to maximize impact and use. While the immediate priority for developing countries is vaccine access and procurement, other priorities should not be forgotten, such as debt sustainability and climate change. Governments across the global south need financial resources to bolster economic recovery, counter wealth and income inequality, and tackle rising poverty.

Recycling Rich Country SDRs

The core inequity in SDR allocation is that they are distributed according to IMF quotas, or financial contribution shares, rather than need. As a result, over 60 percent of SDRs go to a handful of wealthy countries, while developing countries with the greatest need receive the least.

In response, IMF membership asked the institution to explore mechanisms for rich members to voluntarily transfer SDRs to vulnerable countries. Different stakeholders have proposed some forms for such mechanisms, which are not mutually exclusive. For instance: contributing to the IMF Poverty Reduction and Growth Trust facility; financing expanded debt relief through the Catastrophe Containment and Relief Trust; strengthening the financial capacity of multilateral or regional financial institutions; and creating new vehicles - such as the Liquidity and Sustainability Facility, vaccine financing vehicles or the Covid-19 Economic Relief Fund. The key question is how can the design of SDR recycling mechanisms maximize positive impacts for all countries that need support while avoiding harm?

According to Perez Caldentey of ECLAC, recycling SDRs needs to proactively include middle-income countries (MICs). Despite being home to more than 75 percent of the global population, a majority of the world's poor and accounting for almost 96 percent of the external debt of all developing countries (excluding China and India), MICs have so far not been granted access to G20 debt relief. Reallocation, he stressed, should also be used as a way to boost the lending capacity of regional financial institutions and regional banks, such as the FLAR (Fondo Latinoamericano de Reservas) and the Eastern Caribbean Central Bank, among others.

Ocampo emphasized that SDRs should be lent to low- and middle-income countries without conditionality and with attention paid to how exactly to spend the SDRs. For Corbacho at the IMF, the central question is how SDR recycling mechanisms can supplement and meet global reserve needs. The IMF requires broad support from its members, she stressed, as the process of reallocation can only be made effective once the IMF's Executive Board gives its approval.

Donating SDRs

Civil society and many other policy-makers and academics have stressed the importance of maintaining the inherently benign properties of SDRs of being non-debt creating and unconditional. The best way to maintain these properties would be direct donations of SDRs from rich countries to developing countries. However, Ocampo warned that such donations are not easy, as the donating country will have to pay interest on the donated SDRs to the Fund. As a long-term approach to overcome this hurdle, Ocampo proposed this interest should be paid out of the general IMF budget, although he acknowledged that this would be unlikely to occur for this allocation.

Corbacho reiterated the point, noting that the interest costs would be permanently incurred by the donor country. That is why it makes more sense for rich member countries to on-lend their SDRs, rather than donate them. On the other hand, Ghosh countered that the budgetary implications of paying this interest for G7 countries are minor. As such, the issue is convincing rich country governments to agree to donations.

On-lending SDRs

The IMF is reportedly considering its Poverty Reduction and Growth Trust (PRGT) lending facility as a central SDR recycling mechanism. Many civil society advocates have concerns over PRGT loans, however, several of which were mentioned by speakers. The PRGT facility is currently accessible only to LICs and should be made accessible to all developing countries in need, as Ocampo noted. Conditionalities attached to loans, many of which promote fiscal consolidation measures, should be removed, in the same way as the Fund's debt relief scheme for LICs, the Catastrophe Containment and Relief Trust (CCRT), is unconditional, argued Ghosh.

Ghosh underscored that, while the PRGT can provide much-needed liquidity, the emphasis within PRGT loans on cutting fiscal expenditure should be unacceptable in the recycling of SDRs. Ghosh noted that, while IMF leadership and management have made statements that Covid financing should be non-conditional, this point has not yet been incorporated into the Fund's lending facilities.

Countries' Use Of SDRs

Corbacho remarked that SDRs are an unconditional reserve asset that sits on the balance sheets of countries' central banks. It is the IMF's job to advise countries on how to use SDRs transparently and to foster recovery and long-term resilience. But, in her own words "it is up to the members how they will utilize the SDR allocation", a decision which is up "to their best judgement".

Vaccine funds

Songwe emphasized that the priority for the African continent is vaccine access and distribution. As such, as well as supplementing the PRGT, SDRs should be on-lent to create a vaccine fund, Songwe argued. While the priority was to get more countries and companies to produce the vaccine, after production the problem for developing countries would be vaccine affordability. Ghosh stated that SDRs should be specifically recycled into the World Health Organization's Access to Covid-19 Tools (ACT) Accelerator, which addresses diagnostics supplies, personal protection equipment, and medical needs, among other areas.

Corbacho reiterated that ultimately it is up to IMF member countries how they employ unused SDRs. Channeling SDRs for specific purposes such as vaccines and climate change, either through another trust or through Special Purpose Vehicles (SPVs), will need willing creditors as well as satisfying certain criteria, such as the additionality and complementarity of new trusts to existing IMF tools.

A Fund Outside The IMF

Sembene said that, while the IMF is important, it is not the only institution and process by which SDRs can be recycled. Should there be a role for multilateral development banks (MDBs) and mechanisms within these institutions that can leverage SDR resources for use over the long term? Sembene noted that an SDR recycling mechanism that should be brought to the table is on-lending via SPVs that are not yet prescribed holders of SDRs. This would require a decision from the IMF to designate newly prescribed holders of SDRs. He also stressed that one key area that SDR recycling conversations may not be focusing on as much as the role of SDRs in reducing debt burdens across the developing world.

Liquidity And Sustainability Facility

There was debate within the panel on the value of using SDRs to contribute to a Liquidity and Sustainability Facility (LSF) for Africa, which has been proposed by UNECA. The LSF would mobilize private finance for the SDGs through mechanisms such as SDG Covid-19 bonds. According to the ECA, the LSF would be financed by official development assistance, multilateral development banks, and/or by the central banks of members of the Organisation for Economic Co-operation and Development (OECD). The LSF is a response to the African context of sovereign debt, where countries often have to pay higher interest rates than non-African countries with similar macroeconomic fundamentals (often called the 'African premium'), in that the facility hopes to reshape misperceptions about credit risk for African sovereigns.

As Vera Songwe of ECA previously mentioned in a June 2020 Financial Times article, "Africa needs its own repo market, [...] that would attract a new class of investors while shaving off the higher borrowing costs that African nations face because of age-old stubbornly sticky perceptions that they are especially risky." The LSF "modeled on existing market-based and commonly used facilities in Europe and the US [...] would help cut borrowing costs for African governments by providing incentives for the private sector to increase their portfolio investments on the continent."

Ghosh had concerns about these types of facilities for Africa. She noted that, while it was good to leverage existing resources for additional finance, the design of the LSF meant that it was pro-cyclical, dependent on market behavior, and would lead to a loss of the domestic monetary and fiscal policy. Ghosh pointed to the experience of middle-income countries in Asia, which had opened up to bond markets over recent decades and had experienced net losses.

Songwe responded that the LSF was not pro-cyclical and that its role was in correcting market distortions. The LSF is necessary because Africa has not yet deepened its capital markets, meaning that it currently has to borrow at high rates.

A broader discussion of the LSF and its limitations can be found in the Eurodad and partners report The Liquidity and Sustainability Facility for African sovereign bonds: who benefits?

Long-term reforms to maximize the benefits of SDRs An underlying current during the event was a range of voices calling for a more ambitious reformulation of how SDRs can be used to support developing countries. Ocampo identified three long-term solutions. First, eliminating the dual accounting of SDRs - counting as both assets and liabilities - within the IMF's SDR account and its general resources account. In this way, SDRs that have been issued but have not been used by states can be used by the IMF to finance its products. This, for Ocampo, was the most important potential reform. His second proposal was changing the distribution formula for IMF quotas so that the need for foreign reserves is taken into account. This would lead to more SDRs being allocated to low- and middle-income countries. And third, allowing for the private use of SDRs. While these options can move the needle forward for SDRs to achieve their purpose in assisting countries in need, all of them require changes in the IMF's Articles of Agreement, which currently constrains all of these options.

In a similar vein, Ghosh argued that there should be automatic mechanisms within the IMF that keep issuing SDRs over time and that we need to think of reasonable ways of reallocating SDRs to support global public goods. Today we are talking about the pandemic; in the future, it will be climate change. We need cross-border public trusts to ensure some degree of economic resilience, but they cannot be based on the on-lending IMF facilities that are necessarily conditional.

We are all thinking within the constraints of what is possible right now, but ultimately this is no time for business as usual. We need to rethink and step outside of the box if we are to do anything to tackle the massive challenges the global economy is facing today.

Special Drawing Rights: What Are SDRs and How Can They Boost the Global COVID-19 Recovery?

The last time new Special Drawing Rights (SDRs) were issued was during the 2008-2009 financial crisis, unlocking hundreds of billions of dollars to help countries around the world in a time of need.

Now, more than a decade later, world leaders are once again discussing this financing source — this time with hopes that it will help countries recover from the global economic recession brought on by the COVID-19 pandemic.

Below, we break down what SDRs are, how they can boost the global economy, and whose support is needed to tap into this crucial funding, which could be used for medical supplies, vaccines, food, and further debt relief to prevent low-income countries from sliding deeper into poverty.

Created by the International Monetary Fund (IMF) in 1969, the SDR is a reserve asset that can be traded between countries in exchange for liquidity or cash.

Each time the IMF decides to issue a new allocation of SDRs, the organization is acting as an international central bank.

The IMF distributes these reserve assets to its 190 member countries in proportion to their IMF share and relative economic standing in the world economy. So richer countries get more SDRs, while poorer countries receive fewer.

Countries can then buy or sell SDRs depending on their needs. For example, a country that is suffering economically and needs more liquidity to make payments can sell a portion of its SDRs in exchange for cash, especially US dollars or euros. SDRs can also be used to repay the debt a country owes, for instance to the IMF, or can be held as security.

Since the creation of the SDRs after World War II, the IMF has allocated SDR 204.2 billion (equivalent to about $290 billion) to its member countries, including SDR 182.6 billion in 2009 in the wake of the global financial crisis. The 2009 allocation was the most recent and by far the largest.

Renewed Urgency For Special Drawing Rights

In the past year, several world leaders, humanitarian groups, and other experts have voiced support for the issuance of a new SDR allocation as part of the effort to help the international community recover from the pandemic. Such a move would provide extra reserves to each IMF member country at a time when funding needs remain large, especially for low-income countries hit hard by the virus.

This additional financing source would give low-income nations more flexibility and power to address immediate as well as long-term needs arising from the COVID-19 crisis, whether that's purchasing vaccines or revitalizing the workforce and economy.

At a time when economic disparities are widening and the United Nations' Global Goals are falling further from reach, ensuring that governments have the resources to support their most vulnerable populations is crucial.

It will be much more difficult to kick start global growth, end extreme poverty, and get back on track to achieve the Global Goals in the next decade if these vulnerable populations are not accounted for and supported now.

This month, French President Emmanuel Macron, German Chancellor Angela Merkel, European Council President Charles Michel, Senegal's President Macky Sall, UN Secretary-General Antonio Guterres, and European Commission President Ursula von der Leyen published an op-ed that included a call for the use of SDRs to reduce the debt burden and support sustainable recovery in developing countries.

"We need to ensure that the global recovery reaches everybody," they wrote. "That means stepping up our support to developing countries, particularly in Africa, by building on and going beyond existing partnerships..."

Italy, this year's president of the Group of 20 — the world's biggest advanced and emerging economies — will urge the G20 to back the new issuance of SDR 500 billion when they meet in Rome, according to Reuters.

Gelsomina Vigliotti, Italy's treasury director-general for international financial relations, called it "an absolute priority" to make available these additional reserve assets.

"We must grant fiscal space to the low-income countries in greatest difficulty," Vigliotti said. "The goal is to ensure a new allocation of SDRs is made available to the countries most in need."

Under former US President Donald Trump's administration, the US had blocked the idea of a new SDR allocation, saying it would provide more resources to richer countries since allocations are based on countries' IMF shareholding.

However, both Vigliotti and IMF Managing Director Kristalina Georgieva have pointed out that advanced economies that don't need their SDRs can donate their allotment to help developing countries.

In the context of the 2009 financial crisis, the IMF issued a new SDR allocation for similar reasons — to help the international economy recover. Although a smaller number of SDRs went to the IMF's low-income members due to the allocation system, in most cases the process resulted in a proportionately bigger increase in reserves for the poorer countries than for the advanced economies.

"The general SDR allocation is a key part of our response to the global crisis, demonstrating the value of a cooperative multilateral approach," Caroline Atkinson, the IMF's external relations director, said in 2009. "The Fund's low-income members will benefit significantly."

The US has a controlling vote at the IMF on SDR- related decisions, which means if it joined other countries in supporting a new allocation, such financial support could once again help the world recover.

Now with a new US administration under President Joe Biden, there is renewed hope for the passage of an SDR allocation in response to the COVID-19 crisis.

The Biden administration has previously signaled support for a new allocation of SDRs, according to Reuters, but experts and civil society organizations continue to call for urgent action. US Treasury Secretary Janet Yellen is expected to decide by Feb. 26, when the G20 members will meet to discuss the matter further.

CHAPTER 4

Overcoming The Technical And Political Difficulties Of Using SDRs For Development Purposes

The case for using Special Drawing Rights (SDRs), the reserve asset issued by the International Monetary Fund (IMF), for development purposes and the provision of global public goods has originally been made by Soros (2002) and Stiglitz (2003), to transfer unused SDRs from industrial countries to global funds and countries in need of development assistance. This proposal has more recently been revived at the 15th Conference of Parties (COP) of UNFCCC held in Copenhagen in 2009 where George Soros suggested using SDRs to create a global "green fund," The idea was later supported by the previous IMF Managing Director, Dominique Strauss-Kahn, as well as many civil society organizations. Meanwhile, the governor of the People's Bank of China, Zhou Xiochuan, proposed that the SDR should gradually replace the dollar at the center of the international financial system and that surplus countries should be able to convert their holdings of dollar reserves into SDR-denominated assets (Zhou, 2009). Recently, the G20 group of countries expressed great interest in SDR-related ideas and improved the political feasibility of an SDR-facilitated reform agenda. The Commission of Experts on Reforms of the International Monetary and Financial System convened by the President of the UN General Assembly (Stiglitz Commission) suggested regular allocations of SDR in the range of US$150-300 billion a year (United Nations, 2009, ch. 5).

There are two distinct purposes for resuming the allocation of SDRs, the final and largest of which was US$250 billion in 2009. First, SDR allocations reduce the need for precautionary reserve accumulation by providing access to foreign currency liquidity, thus acting essentially as a swap line. As a lower-cost alternative to accumulating international reserves through borrowing or building up to current account surpluses, the SDR would reduce the costs of self-insurance against currency crises for many developing countries. This can be referred to as the "international liquidity purpose" of SDR allocations. Second, regular SDR allocations can form a potential source of development finance. Through SDR allocations, the seigniorage related to additional demand for global currencies accrues to the IMF member states. In proportion to IMF quotas, more than half of SDR allocations are distributed to industrial countries. The remainder of the SDR allocations accrues to developing countries, and this creates the potential for the international seigniorage to provide resources of comparable or even higher levels of ODA.

While the "international liquidity purpose" creates an incentive to reduce self-insuring reserve accumulation, the function of raising additional development finance allows for the redistribution of international seigniorage to the provisioning of global public goods and financing to countries facing high costs of borrowing in world capital markets. Having set forth the distinction between the monetary and development finance functions of SDR, this paper focuses on the development finance function.

The rest of the paper is organized as follows. The next section discusses the problems of the current international reserve system and evaluates the potential of different paths of reform to solve these problems. The following section focuses on the estimates of SDR allocations in the literature, provides an updated estimate, and discusses their potential for development finance. The next two sections address the technical and political difficulties of implementing an SDR-based system and explore different ways to overcome them. The section following deals with complementary reforms necessary for the SDR-based system to work and the final section draws major conclusions.

International Reserve System: Multi-Currency or SDR-Based?

The unilateral decision of the USA in 1971 to abandon the gold-dollar parity was a critical milestone marking the end of the Bretton Woods system and paving the way for the current reserve system centered on a "fiduciary dollar standard" (Ocampo, 2010a) or a "semi-dollar standard" (Aglietta, 2010). Table 1 shows that in 2010 about 61.5 percent of foreign exchange reserves were held in US dollars while the share of euros followed with 26.2 percent and other currencies such as yen and sterling with 12.3 percent. Many had expected that the euro would pose a major challenge to the dollar as the global reserve currency. However, that did not happen. The share of euro-area currencies in 1995 was slightly higher than the 2010 share of euro in foreign exchange reserves, and the rise of the share of euro from 1999 to 2010 is attributable to the appreciation of the euro against the dollar during this period. In other words, the US dollar does not face any effective competition against its dominant role as a global reserve asset, and the problems of sovereign debt in the euro area make the prospects of a rising share of the euro less likely.

The scale of foreign exchange reserves accumulated in 2010 was more than US$9 trillion (see Table 1). Emerging and developing countries held about two-thirds of these reserves: slightly more than US$6 trillion. The share of US dollars in their reserves declined from 74.3 percent in 1999 to 58.3 percent in 2010—that is, more than half of their reserves are still held in US dollars2.

The reserve accumulation in developing countries has risen sharply since the 1990s and diverged from the advanced country trends. Figure 1 shows that the foreign exchange reserves of low-income and middle-income countries were similar to those of high-income countries in the 1980s, around 3-4 percent of GDP. The initial point of divergence took place in the 1990s following the emerging country crises and intensified after the 1997-8 East Asian crisis. Many developing countries sought instruments to protect themselves against global financial instability and to manage pro-cyclical capital flows. Together with the intentions to avoid conditionalities associated with IMF lending, this generated a massive accumulation of reserves—which in fact imply transfers of resources to reserve-issuing countries. The end result is a flow of vast amounts of resources from the developing world to industrialized countries issuing reserve currencies. This unequal flow of resources from those who need them the most to those that already have plenty has been referred to as the "inequity bias" in the international monetary system (Ocampo 2011).

Imperfections of the International Monetary System

Imperfections of the current international monetary system are frequently emphasized and can be grouped under three categories (see Ocampo, 2011; CEPII, 2011; Padoa-Schioppa, 2011). First, the system has an in- equity bias reflected in the growing needs of the developing countries to accumulate foreign exchange reserves. This self-insurance policy has serious downsides. First, it reflects a lack of trust in multilateral mechanisms resulting in large-scale investment in reserve assets with low yields. The difference between these yield rates and the interest rate that developing countries pay to industrial countries when they borrow from them is a transfer of resources greater than the value of ODA. Second, self-insurance suffers from a fallacy of composition: the simultaneous pursuit of current account surpluses or small current account deficits by a large number of countries contribute to the widening of global imbalances.

The second imperfection of the international monetary system is widely known as the Triffin Dilemma named after the Belgian economist Robert Triffin. This emerges from the use of a national currency (the US dollar) as the international reserve currency. The dilemma is that either the world has to suffer from a lack of liquidity if the supply of the reserve asset is constrained (if the US aims to reduce its current account deficits or capital account surpluses), or the increasing deficits of the reserve-issuing country will eventually undermine the value of the reserve currency and lead to a breakdown of the system. The strategy of reserve accumulation is only sustainable if there is at least one reserve-issuing country large enough and willing to run ever-larger current account deficits or capital account surpluses to ensure sufficient liquidity for global economic activities.

However, the rising deficits of the reserve-issuing country tend to erode confidence in the reserve currency and create a risk of loss in the value of foreign exchange reserves held in this currency.

The third imperfection of the current monetary system is the asymmetric adjustment that it places on a deficit and surplus countries. The countries in external surplus have no incentive to adjust, and due to the international role of the dollar, the United States has no incentive to adjust when it is in deficit. The burden of adjustment falls onto non-dominant deficit countries, but it takes place with a long lag and rather abruptly when deficit financing suddenly dries out, creating unnecessary macroeconomic instability.

Multi-Currency Reserve System versus SDR-Based Reserve System

Fundamental reform of the global reserve system is necessary to overcome these interrelated imperfections. There are two paths of reform discussed widely. The first one is to improve the multi-currency nature of the current system with multiple reserve currencies competing against each other. This would require an increase in the use of other currencies such as the euro and renminbi. While the Europeans are enthusiastic about promoting the euro as a reserve asset (see a recent report by Cepii, 2011), the recent debt crisis indicated that the backing from a heterogeneous set of countries without a fiscal union makes the euro a rather imperfect substitute for the dollar. Meanwhile, the internationalization of the renminbi is gaining pace with the emphasis Chinese authorities put on Hong Kong as a hub for renminbi-denominated asset transactions. However, China's financial markets are not well-developed and the renminbi is not fully convertible, which limits carrying out global transactions in this currency while making it less vulnerable to speculative attacks. For the renminbi to become a reserve asset, it would be important to have full convertibility for central banks that hold renminbi.

The multi-currency reserve system fails, however, to resolve imperfections of the current reserve system. First, it will require national currencies, most of which will still be currencies of major industrial countries, to be used as reserve assets. The Triffin Dilemma would then apply to the group of reserve currency countries which would have to run increasing current account deficits (or capital account surpluses) to supply the world with reserve currencies. Secondly, the diversification of reserve accumulation would come at the cost of exchange rate volatility among reserve currencies. Since none of these currencies will have stable values due to their floating nature, the central banks would respond by changing the composition of their assets, which can be rather costly if their predictions about future movements in the exchange rates turn out to be incorrect. Ocampo (2011) suggested that the multi-currency solution would require an IMF substitution account, an element of the SDR-based reform proposed in this paper, to stabilize the exchange rate fluctuations. Third, it would not solve the inequity bias of the current system, since most developing countries would still be investing their savings into reserve assets issued by industrial countries. Lastly, the multi-currency system would not put pressure on surplus countries to adjust, and therefore, continue to suffer from asymmetric adjustment problems.

The alternative path is to design a global currency as a reserve asset initially and to use it as a means of payment later. This reform path can be implemented by one of the following institutions: (i) a new institution created to function as a Global Reserve Bank, (ii) an existing network of regional institutions, or (iii) the IMF (United Nations, 2009). The first option involves negotiations for a new global institution, which would not only be time-consuming but also politically difficult to agree upon. The second and third options are complementary parts of an SDR-based reform of the global reserve system. Since the IMF is currently the only institution issuing a global currency, the SDRs, the reserve system can be built on it and supported by a network of regional arrangements such as reserve- pooling institutions including the Chiang Mai Initiative, the Latin American Reserve Fund, and the Arab Monetary Fund.

Estimates of SDR Allocations and their Potential for Development Finance

As a response to the global crisis, the G-20 and the IMF members agreed on the allocation of US$250 billion worth of SDRs in April 2009. Despite this extraordinary allocation, the volume of total outstanding SDRs is 204 billion, which is less than 4 percent of global reserves. Partly due to this small share, the countries holding SDRs hardly trade them to pursue any developmental objectives. Instead, many countries meet their growing demand for reserves by accumulating current account surpluses, which places deflationary pressure on the already demand-constrained world economy. The faster growth of demand for international reserves in relation to their supply creates an urgent need for larger allocations of SDRs not only for diversification of their reserve accumulation but also as a potential source of development finance.

Previous Estimates of SDR Allocations

As provided a list of studies that proposed a regular allocation of SDRs, their methods of estimation, and the amounts of issuance estimated. Regardless of differences in estimation techniques, it is seen that recent studies propose a consistent amount of regular allocations ranging from an average of US$200-300 billion annually. This would result in a significant diversification of reserves. For example, the IMF (2011) estimated that an annual allocation of US$200 billion would increase the share of SDRs in total reserves to about 13 percent by 2020s.

Generally, in proposing the amount of SDR to be issued, studies rely on an indicator of global demand for additional reserves with a precautionary motive. Given that over 2003-08 the average annual holdings of reserves increased by US$737 billion or US$370 billion excluding China and Japan, Ocampo (2011) suggests an allocation of US$250-300 billion a year as a reasonable estimate. The Commission of Experts on Reforms of the International Monetary and Financial System convened by the President of the UN General Assembly (Stiglitz Commission) proposed a similar estimate, US$150-300 billion annually, with the average annual reserve accumulation in 1998-2002 as lower bound, and that in 2003-07 as upper bound. A more recent recommendation by a group of experts including Stiglitz is, however, much larger -US$240-400 billion (Stiglitz et al. 2011).

It is important to note that the Soros proposal differs from the rest in its one-time lending from developed countries to a green fund that serves the developing world. Arguing that more than $150 billion of the recently allocated SDRs went to the 15 largest developed economies, which could lend two-thirds of this amount to a green fund for 25 years, Soros emphasized this potential means to fund climate change mitigation. However, the proposal faces several obstacles before it can be implemented. Most importantly, this requires the SDRs, which are strictly monetary assets of central banks, to be used for fiscal purposes. Their fiscal use would have to be approved by national parliaments and it could be legally complicated to make fiscal use of what is strictly a central bank asset (Ocampo and Griffith-Jones, 2011).

To ensure a stable source of liquidity in world markets, the SDRs should be allocated on a counter-cyclical basis. This means increasing the supply of SDRs in periods of global financial difficulties and reducing their supply by partly destroying them when financial markets become more stable. Such counter-cyclical allocations are crucial to offsetting any inflationary pressures that might otherwise arise.

An Estimate of SDR Allocations

It is possible to estimate a range for the regular allocation of SDRs based on the most recent data available. The world demand for additional reserves in 2000-05 was on average US$246 billion, but it has since then almost doubled. In 2006-10 the world demand for reserves was US$443 billion (Table 3). Thus, the recent recommendation of analysts including Stiglitz et al. (2011) for annual allocations ranging from US$240-400 billion is in fact a rather reasonable estimate that is endorsed here. Indeed, since the estimations exclude outliers of Japan and China, they can be considered quite conservative and they might err on the side of underestimation instead of overestimation.

SDR Allocations and Development Finance

The extent to which these SDR allocations are directed to development finance requires considering a set of additional problems. First, there is a separation in the accounts of the IMF between the "general resources" and the SDR accounts, which restricts the use of SDR allocations. Under the current IMF Articles of The agreement, it is not possible to use these allocations for financing IMF lending. This problem can be overcome with a change in the current rules that will make the SDRs the major form of financing of IMF lending. As emphasized by the Stiglitz Commission and Ocampo (2011), the unused SDRs, especially from industrial countries, could be treated as deposits in the IMF, which uses these funds to finance its lending to member countries in need.

Second, since SDRs are an international reserve asset that can only be used by central banks under the current rules, their allocation for development purposes or global public goods means that they have to be donated or transferred to a central bank or an international financial institution, which can also hold SDRs. The allocation of SDRs for specific spending purposes (such as funding developmental projects) essentially entails them to be used as a fiscal instrument, which goes beyond their function as strictly monetary instruments. A number of analysts emphasized that the fiscal use of SDRs can create problems in practice because each time they would have to be approved in national parliaments and that it might even be legally problematic to make fiscal use of a central bank asset (Ocampo, 2011). The allocation of SDRs for any fiscal use could only be possible with changes in the IMF Articles of Agreement.

A "development link" in SDR allocations has been proposed by Ocampo (2011), which avoids the SDR allocations for development to be treated as a financial transaction. The IMF would use the unutilized SDRs of the member states to buy bonds from multilateral development banks, which would in turn finance development and global public goods. The idea is similar to that suggested by the Group of Experts convened by UNCTAD in the 1960s (UNCTAD 1965) and it is recently supported by the Stiglitz Commission (2009). If the bonds are offered at market rates, their use by multilateral banks would be non-concessional. It might, however, be possible to combine this form of lending with revenues from a currency transactions tax or more traditional grants, in which case the bonds that IMF buys from multilateral development banks can assist in financing concessional forms of lending as well.

If this "development link" is approved by the G-20 and the IMF, the outcome for estimated development finance could be proportional to unused SDRs allocated to industrial countries. If the IMF goes with the estimated figure of US$240-400 billion annual allocations, the funds going to industrial countries would be over US$144-240 billion and a conservative estimate of US$100-200 billion would be unutilized funds. The amount - US$100-200 billion - could be used by the IMF to buy bonds from multilateral development banks to finance development and/or global public goods.

A third issue that needs to be addressed is the fact that SDR allocations are based on existing quotas at the IMF, which do not reflect the shares of different countries in the global economy. Developing countries are under-represented based on their share of global GDP, which means that a large portion of any new allocations of SDRs is issued to industrial countries. This fact strengthens the inequity bias given that it is the developing countries that have the greatest demand for reserves. To overcome this problem, there is a need to reform quota allocations at the IMF regularly to reflect the changing shares of emerging countries in the world economy.

A way to go around this quota reallocation problem is to issue SDRs asymmetrically, in which case a larger share of allocations would be issued to emerging and developing countries given that their demand for reserves is the highest among all. For example, since these countries currently hold about 80 percent of all international reserves, they could receive 80 percent of SDR allocations and the remaining 20 percent could be allocated to industrial countries (Williamson, 2010). Allocations within each group would be determined by each country's quota at the IMF. If the IMF allocates US$240-400 billion worth of SDRs annually according to the 80-20 rule suggested, the developing countries would be issued US$192-320 billion, and each developing country would receive a share of this amount according to its quota share. How much of these funds would be allocated for development finance? Each country could draw the funds they need to finance their development needs, and the cost would be the foregone interest earned on holding these SDR allocations at the IMF. However, note that the fiscal use of SDRs is not currently allowed within the current IMF rules, and there is a need for reform if this asymmetric issuance is going to increase development finance. One benefit of asymmetric SDRs allocation is a gradual diversification of developing countries away from the US dollar as an international reserve asset. In this regard, it eliminates or reduces the transfer of resources from developing to industrial countries, i.e. the inequity bias. By delinking the international reserve asset from any particular national currency, the SDR allocations also overcome the Triffin dilemma.

Technical Difficulties

In the transition towards an SDR-based reserve system, one of the technical difficulties that IMF faces is the creation of a "substitution account," which allows countries to exchange their dollar reserves and those denominated in other currencies for the SDRs and SDR-denominated assets issued by the Fund. This would bring the benefit of preventing an abrupt depreciation of the dollar if the large-holders of dollar reserves try to sell them in the foreign exchange market. In this sense, the substitution account would be essential to maintain the stability in exchange rate movements, and it would be also highly useful in a multi-currency arrangement to prevent excessive volatility. These benefits should be weighed against the costs of a substitution account that focuses on the crucial question of "who bears the exchange rate risk?" This section will review the benefits of having a substitution account and evaluate its costs based on different options to share the exchange rate risk.

Benefits of a Substitution Account

Establishing a substitution account at the IMF to allow the countries that hold US dollar (or other currency) reserves to diversify into SDRs brings many benefits. Although difficult to quantify, two of the benefits are essential to show the desirability of its creation:

Altering The Composition Of Reserves Without Disruption

The developing and emerging countries hold US\$6.1 trillion worth of foreign exchange reserves, about US\$5 trillion of which is held in US dollars. Clearly, with a reserve accumulation of about US\$3 trillion, China has the largest need to diversify its reserves accumulated in US dollars and invested in US government securities. This desire was expressed clearly by the governor of the People's Bank of China, Zhou Xiochuan, who proposed that surplus countries should be able to convert their holdings of dollar reserves into SDR-denominated assets (Zhou, 2009). If China sells these reserves in the foreign exchange market, the value of the dollar would collapse, creating a dollar crisis. The substitution account would prevent this crisis by allowing the dollar reserves to be exchanged with SDRs in an off-market reserve pool. In this sense, the substitution account would allow a timely diversification for countries holding excess dollar reserves. It is also important to emphasize that China is not alone in trying to diversify. Many developing countries in

East Asia, South Asia, and the Middle East accumulated excessive amounts of reserves to self-insure against crises and would benefit from a diversification mechanism away from the US dollar whose value might deteriorate over time due to structural factors.

Acting As A First Step In The Transition Towards An SDR-Based Reserve System

By allowing countries to transform their dollar reserves or reserves denominated in other currencies into SDR-denominated assets in an off-market reserve pool, the creation of a substitution account is the first step toward a substantial reform of the international reserve system. The main advantage would be the stability that it provides to the system, and it would also be crucial to manage exchange rate volatility generated in a multi-currency system. Similar to the three-stage transition envisioned by Kenen (2010b), one can think of three periods in which the functions of the substitution account change to eventually transform the SDR into a fully developed reserve asset. In the earlier period after which the substitution account is established, the potential costs arising from maintaining the value of the reserves deposited in the account can be shared between the reserve-issuers (the United States and the Eurozone countries) and the reserve-holders (the majority being developing and emerging countries). During this period, the IMF would continue making periodic SDR allocations to its members, which would be deposited in the substitution account. In the subsequent period, each county that needs to intervene in the foreign exchange market would be able to freely transfer some of its SDR claims on the substitution account to the country issuing the currency that it needs to access. For example, if India needs to have dollars to intervene in the foreign exchange market, it would transfer some of its SDRs to the United States in exchange for dollars at the prevailing dollar-SDR exchange rate. In the final phase, the substitution account can be consolidated with the SDR department of the IMF and any distinction between the SDRs created through substitution and SDRs created by periodic allocations would disappear. The free transferability of SDRs in exchange for other currencies would be extended to all members of the IMF including the countries that had not initially deposited any reserves into the substitution account. This would allow the SDR to become a fully developed international reserve asset, providing stability and adjustment to the global reserve system.

Costs of a Substitution Account

The creation of a substitution account within the IMF was previously debated in the late 1970s, but the negotiations failed for two reasons: (i) the US dollar began to revalue in the early 1980s, which offset the fears of dollar reserves losing value, and (ii) the United States refused to take responsibility as the single country to sustain the dollar value of the SDR- denominated assets in the substitution account.

These two factors still exist in today's world. The US dollar began to strengthen recently in response to the deepening of the Eurozone debt crisis and the haven status of the dollar. The strengthening of the dollar was so much that many emerging countries (such as Brazil, Turkey, India) had to intervene to prevent the depreciation of their currencies while their earlier worries were all about appreciation. The second factor is also present given that the United States is unlikely to accept an arrangement in which it would be wholly responsible for the solvency of the account.

However, there are two ways to overcome these opposing forces. First, it should be recognized that even if the US dollar becomes strong during this ongoing crisis, there is no guarantee that it will be able to keep its strength for the following periods given its growing debt problem and current account deficits. Thus, for the benefit of all countries holding their reserves in dollar-denominated assets, there is a need to convert them into

SDRs through the substitution account without causing the dollar to depreciate against other major currencies. This would also benefit the United States whose currency will not face an unexpected and sudden depreciation if the substitution account functions properly.

Second, there are mechanisms in which the potential costs of the substitution account can be shared among the IMF members or large surplus countries such as China, Japan, and Germany. These cost-sharing mechanisms would take the burden from the United States and distribute it over a broader range of countries.

Kenen (2010b) provided historical simulations of how much the potential costs of keeping the account solvent would be and what kind of cost-sharing mechanisms would make the substitution account a viable arrangement. His simulation results vary based on (i) which year is chosen as the first year in which the account begins to function, (ii) how much is deposited in the first year, (ii) what kinds of shocks are chosen to see the impact of changes in interest rates and exchange rates, and (iv) which cost-sharing mechanisms are implemented.

The first factor, for example, shows a large variation in cost estimates. If the year 1980 is chosen as the first year for the creation of the account starting with a deposit of US$500 billion, the average annual deficiency payment, or the cost of keeping the account solvent, would be US$22.6 billion, or if it is spread over the whole 29-year period, the average annual cost would be US$16.4 billion, which could be paid with a cost-sharing mechanism between the United States and the countries depositing their reserves. However, if the first year is chosen to be 1995 and the initial deposit is assumed to be US$1000 billion, the historical simulation results show that the total cost turns out to be zero, i.e. there would be no deficiency costs as the total value of dollar amount equals the total dollar value of the SDR amount in the substitution account for every year. Application of various shocks to this base-case scenario results in various estimates of deficiency payments, ranging from US$322-586 billion, which are way above the base-case scenario's figures in 1980.

To overcome the problem of which party has to pay for these costs once and for all, one should pay attention to the fact that the substitution account holds surplus dollars many years before it gets into a deficit situation requiring deficiency payments. That is, it alternates between periods of surplus and deficit in terms of dollars. This calls for a "counterpart account" to be established in the United States (or in the IMF as an additional account) which would be credited when the substitution account is in surplus and debited when it is in deficit. The simulations show that the accumulated credited amounts would balance out the accumulated deficits over time, making the problem of which country pays for it effectively a non-problem.

At present a US interest rate shock of a 1 percentage point decline in 2000 to the base-case scenario of 1995 considered in Kenen (2010b). It is important to note that the balance on the substitution account is explicitly shown here whereas it was omitted in Kenen (2010b). The balance on the substitution account, which is the difference between the dollar amount in the account and the dollar value of the SDR amount is positive for all years except 2004 and 2007. That is, the account is in surplus except for these two years, and the sum of these surplus years is US$1,219.57 billion, which is much larger than the sum of two deficit years (US$112.34 billion). A counterpart account could be used to balance these two items in which case the net cost could be zero—in fact, there would be a positive balance in the end. Otherwise, the sum of deficits amounts to the deficiency payments and their accumulation together with interest charges yields a figure of US$119.53 that has to be paid either by the United States or by a cost-sharing mechanism between the

United States and depositors of US dollars into IMF substitution account.

One way to share these costs in the absence of a counterpart account would be to divide the total deficiency payments between the United States and the IMF, each paying half of the total. The IMF can use its own dollar holdings or sell some of its gold holdings to share in the cost of holding the substitution account solvent. Another cost-sharing mechanism could be to identify those countries that would benefit by far the most (i.e. the largest surplus countries such as China, Japan, Germany) from having a substitution account in the IMF and ask these countries to carry more responsibility in sharing the costs. A G-20 summit might be a good venue to reach an agreement about how the potential costs of the substitution account might be shared. For example, it can be made proportional to the shares of dollar deposits into the account from each country. The owners of larger shares would then share a larger part of the potential cost.

Another mechanism that puts the entire responsibility on the depositors would be to put the IMF in charge of collecting an annual fee of 1 percent of the dollar reserves deposited in the account at the end of each year. These annual fees would be deposited to a Substitution Account Reserve Fund (SARF), which would in- vest them in US government securities. This would allow the size of the SARF to grow in a compound fashion, and the accumulated amount can later be used to pay for deficits in the account. In case of insufficiency of SARF dollar assets to cover deficits, the SARF could borrow from the IMF and pay back from the following receipts of annual fees. This is the proposal advocated by Kenen (2010b, p. 11-12), who adds that this arrangement could be modified in two ways: (i) the costs can be divided between the United States and the depositors, and (ii) the SARF can borrow from the United States, instead of the IMF, if its dollar assets are insufficient.

A modified version of this proposal could be based on sharing the costs of keeping the substitution account solvent. For example, the SARF and the United States can share the cost equally, each paying half of the deficiency payments required. The cost-sharing ratios might change depending on how much the total SARF dollar assets will be accumulated. That is, if the total amount becomes easily as large as any deficiency payment required, the United States might only step in when there is an excessive rise in the deficit. In the case of an interest rate shock, annual contributions of 1% of total dollar reserves would amount to US$108.6 billion by the end of 2004 and US$150.7 billion at the end of 2007, both of which are large enough to compensate for the deficiency payments required (US$69.4 and US$42.9 billion respectively). However, if the simulation begins in 1980, it is seen that the SARF would be in deficit in the 1990s and would have to borrow from the IMF or the United States, depending on the final arrangement.

In order to determine the cost of holding the substitution account solvent, so far we have only considered a decline in the US interest rate. Two more shocks might be important in estimating the cost: (i) a rise in the SDR interest rate, and (ii) a depreciation of the US dollar. The historical simulation for the SDR interest rate increased 1 percentage point in the year 2000. Also there are two years with deficits (2004 and 2007) while the rest of the time there is a surplus in the account. The total surplus in the account (US$1,241.96 billion) is again far greater than the total deficit (US$118.34). This means that in the presence of a counterpart account in the United States or the IMF, the total cost would have been zero. If there is no counterpart account in place, the total cost to be shared among the United States and the depositors would be US$129.43 at the end of 2008. Depending on the cost-sharing mechanism, this amount could either be paid completely by the depositors, by the United States, or by both, as each party assumes a certain share of the cost.

And the historical simulations of the cases in which the US dollar depreciates by 10 percent and 20 percent respectively. In both cases, it is clear that a counterpart account would balance the account since the total surplus is greater than the total deficit, which would enable the total cost to be equal to zero. However, in the absence of such an account, the total cost amounts to US$13.70 billion if the dollar depreciates by 10 percent, whereas it increases to US$321.96 billion if the dollar depreciates by 20 percent. The comparison indicates the importance of the degree to which the dollar depreciates in determining what the cost of holding the substitution account solvent would be.

The worst-case scenario that Kenen (2010b) considers is the case in which all of these shocks happen at the same time: the US interest rate declines by 1 percentage point, the SDR interest rate increases by 1 percentage point, and the US dollar depreciates by 20 percent. This is a highly unrealistic scenario because it assumes that the non-dollar interest rates that determine the SDR interest rate increase while the US interest rate declines simultaneously. The total cost in the worst-case scenario would be US$586.2 billion, which corresponds to 3 percent of total US foreign assets and 4.1 percent of US GDP in 2008. In terms of average annual cost, this would be equivalent to 0.2 percent of total US foreign assets and 0.3 percent of US GDP in 2008 (Kenen 2010b, p. 8). That is, the costs of maintaining the solvency of the substitution account are negligible in terms of the size of the total US foreign assets and US GDP, and it would even be much smaller if there is a cost-sharing mechanism in which the US pays only half (or less than half) of this amount, depending on the arrangement.

Inflation Versus Deflation Effects Of SDRs

It is important to consider whether the creation of new central bank money in the form of SDRs would be inflationary or not. Counter-cyclical financing and allocations by the IMF are two mechanisms that would prevent new SDR allocations to have an inflationary impact.

As suggested by the IMF economist Jacques Polak, the IMF can switch to a fully SDR-funded system, lending the countries in need with newly created SDRs during crises and destroying these SDRs when they pay back the loans (Polak 1979). Such a counter-cyclical financing mechanism would help stabilize the world liquidity level, enhancing global macroeconomic stability. This could be complemented by counter-cyclical allocations of new SDRs by the IMF, focusing their issuance in periods of financial turmoil and economic recession and partially eliminating them when the economy recovers from the crisis (Ocampo 2011). Another principle for new SDR allocations is to regularly allocate SDRs as a fraction of the additional world demand for reserves, which was discussed in the previous sections. In this case, there is no money created unless countries sell their SDR assets to countries that issue freely usable currencies. Even if they exchanged SDRs for these currencies, the relevant central banks can sterilize any undesired money creation. As long as new SDR allocations are not made in times of strong global demand and inflationary concerns and the central banks sterilize any undesired money creation, the inflationary impact of SDR allocations is expected to be rather limited.

SDR Basket Composition

Another important debate has been whether other currencies can be added to the SDR basket to make it more representative of the composition of world output, trade, and financial transactions. Given the rising share of China in the world's trading and financial system, the central focus of the debate has been whether the renminbi should be included in the SDR basket composition. Including a non-convertible currency such as the renminbi would enable asset holders to gain exposure to these currencies. However, it could also reduce the demand for SDRs for those countries that prefer to hold only convertible currencies. The benefit of including more countries in the basket is not only a better representation of their growing importance in the world economy but also lower volatility of the basket in terms of variance and standard deviation.

The Executive Board of the IMF reviews the SDR basket composition every five years and includes in the basket currencies meeting two criteria: 1) they should be issued by the largest exporters, and 2) they should be freely usable. It is important to note that the IMF does not use the term "fully convertible," but "freely usable" which implies that it is freely usable for payments, settlements of trade, and some FDI investments. Thus, a currency might be considered freely usable even though it is not fully convertible in private markets.

Currently, the SDR basket is composed of 44% US dollar, 34% euro, 11% Japanese yen, and 11%-pound sterling. In broadening the SDR basket, the BRIC countries with their large export share are obvious candidates, but the question arises whether their currencies are freely usable. In this context, it is important to recognize that many currencies were not fully convertible when they were first introduced into the SDR basket. Thus, the partial convertibility of the renminbi should not be an issue as long as the central bank guarantees the convertibility of the renminbi in official transactions.

There are also some reservations about the inclusion of renminbi into the SDR basket. Most notably, the move towards making the renminbi a fully usable currency in private markets would involve liberalizing foreign exchange controls and liberalizing financial and capital markets. This policy shift generates the fear that China might be exposed to volatile capital flows and their destabilizing impacts as in the case of the East Asian crisis. Yet analysts agree that China takes a gradual approach in pursuing capital account liberalization that will culminate in the creation of the Shanghai International Financial Center by 2020 (Ikawa 2009, p. 678). The increasing internationalization of the renminbi is on the agenda of the

Chinese Government as a gradual transformation to prevent any vulnerable exposure to volatile capital flows.

SDR-denominated Bonds

The IMF began issuing bonds denominated in SDRs in 2009, and currently, it has issued SDR 3.2 billion in notes to the official sector with a floating interest and signed notes purchased agreements for SDR 45 billion (IMF, 2011). The IMF had already a framework to issue bonds that were approved in the early 1980 but were never used before 2009. When the IMF began facing cash flow problems in financing its administrative costs in 2008, the proposal to issue bonds was revived. In 2009, the SDR-denominated bonds became a mechanism to increase the resource base of IMF in order to scale up its emergency financing particularly to Eastern European countries.

SDR-denominated bonds were designed to be traded only between IMF and the central banks of its members. As such, there is no secondary market in which private investors could trade these bonds. As the bonds are denominated in SDRs, they pay an interest rate linked to the SDR interest rate, which is composed of the interest rates linked to its composition. The maturity of the bonds is short, ranging from 12-18 months.

The SDR-denominated bonds bring many advantages for developing and emerging countries. First, they reduce the dependence of central banks on U.S. government securities. The developing countries could simply substitute U.S. treasury bills for SDR- denominated bonds by investing in these bonds. A second advantage is that buying these bonds with accumulated foreign exchange reserves does not require any budgetary or legislative approval. Linked to this property, a third advantage is that developing countries will be able to diversify the currency composition of their reserve holdings as the SDR itself is composed of four different currencies. As long as the interest rates earned by government securities of UK, Japan, and the Eurozone countries are higher than the U.S. treasury bills (as is currently the case), the SDR interest rate will be higher than the rate on U.S. treasury bills, making the SDR-denominated bonds more attractive for official investors. Last but not the least, the SDR-denominated bonds allow the developing countries to limit their financial support for the IMF to a particular period, instead of an open-ended commitment through the New Agreements to Borrow (NAB). This limitation provides leverage for the developing countries to push further quota reforms that represent them more evenly in return for making their contributions less temporary (Prasad 2009).

Issuing bonds provide the IMF with more expanded resources, with which it could deal with ongoing crises more effectively. With the highest demand for safe assets in the current financial turmoil, the expansion of the SDR-denominated bond market would be easily achieved and it would be a great service to calm down financial distress since the bonds are backed not only by a single government but by all member states of the IMF. To create market depth and liquidity, the SDR- denominated bonds should be also sold to private investors, who under current rules cannot buy or trade these instruments. It would, therefore, be necessary to change the current Articles and clarify the maturity structure of the bonds and the design of appropriate safeguards to prevent conflicts of interest associated with the Fund's financing role and its new role as global borrower and investor of borrowed resources. In the long-term, once sufficient market depth and liquidity are established, the SDR-denominated securities could replace other global assets in pricing risk globally, and thereby become "an embryo of global currency" (IMF 2011).

The Absence Of Private Markets For SDRs

Some analysts have found the SDR-based reform of the reserve system limited because a major boost to the role of the SDR relies on its transformation into an asset held by the private sector (Cooper 2009, Eichengreen 2009). The private use of SDRs is certainly necessary for the SDR to compete with the dollar in private transactions. If the private actors are not even allowed to hold SDRs, it is hard to imagine how the SDR could replace the dollar in private markets.

The absence of private markets for SDR use does not, however, prevent its use as a central bank asset in reserve accumulation and debt settlement processes. As long as central banks agree to accept SDRs from one another in exchange for convertible currencies, the SDR performs the function of a medium of exchange in inter-central bank transactions. The real issue is whether a central bank can use SDRs to intervene in the foreign exchange market. The inability to do so in the earlier period of reform creates an inconvenience that raises the question of whether SDRs are a better asset for central banks to hold (Williamson 2009).

This inconvenience can nevertheless be overcome if the free transferability of SDRs to issuers of demanded currencies in exchange for these currencies at the prevailing exchange rate is guaranteed. Each IMF member has to guarantee the obligation to freely accept SDRs in exchange for their currencies. As Kenen (2010b) discussed, this obligation can be accepted by members in the second stage of reform which comes after the regular and large-scale allocations of SDRs by the IMF and their increased use as reserve assets, and it can take a decade to accomplish this initial phase. Once this phase is completed, the transition to the second stage would then allow each country to access any currency they need freely by transferring their SDRs, after which they can intervene in the foreign exchange markets to modify their exchange rates. Therefore, the absence of private markets for SDRs would no longer be an obstacle to their use in foreign exchange market intervention.

Political Difficulties

The SDR-based reform of the global reserve system has to take into consideration the political difficulties and ways to reconcile them. It is well-known that the failure of the SDR to play a major role in the late 1970s was due to the unwillingness of the United States to guarantee the solvency of the substitution account as it would place the whole burden of exchange rate risk as well as less costly interest rate risks on this country. To avoid the same kind of failure to reach an agreement, it is therefore essential to design a cost-sharing mechanism that distributes the potential costs among the countries participating in the substitution account. Different types of cost-sharing mechanisms are evaluated in the previous section. In what follows we will consider the interests of the United States and the developing countries to find common grounds that can form the basis of agreement for the reserve system reform.

United States Interests

It is commonly assumed that the United States has a strong national interest against the enhanced role of the SDR since this enhancement might come at the cost of restraining the dollar's international use. The situation is, however, more of a trade-off between two opposing influences:

1) The United States gains from international acceptance of the dollar and its reserve asset status by reducing its cost of borrowing, financing its foreign debt more cheaply, and its ability to thereby conduct strong counter-cyclical macroeconomic policies. This means that the United States is better off due to the seigniorage benefits that accrue to it. It can achieve this benefit by the "exorbitant privilege" of issuing a reserve currency as foreign official holders demand the dollar.

2) It loses by the increasing current account deficits that have adverse effects on the U.S. domestic demand. In order to offset this reduction in domestic demand, the U.S. has to maintain persistent expansionary fiscal and/or monetary policies that would lead to increased public and/or private in- indebtedness. These twin deficits require the periodic

use of contractionary policies that in turn depress the U.S. economy.

The seigniorage benefits derived from the international acceptance of the dollar come at the cost of larger external deficits and higher levels of debt that encourage capital flight and create adverse effects on the U.S. economy. Another disadvantage of having the dollar as the reserve currency is the risk of losing monetary policy autonomy if the United States has to respond to the demands of major holders of the dollar reserves in U.S. government debt by not pursuing policies that would result in the depreciation of the dollar. Thus, if the U.S. desires to keep its monetary policy autonomy coupled with a reduction in its twin deficits and overall indebtedness, the transition to an SDR-based reserve system that promotes global financial and economic stability is in its best interest. It is also important to keep in mind that the confidence in the dollar as a reserve currency seems to be eroding (given the depreciative impact of U.S. expansionary monetary policy), and this erosion would restrain the ability of the U.S. to continue borrowing at low-interest rates.

In the transition process, it will be essential to enhance the role of SDRs first only as a reserve asset by limiting its holding to central banks and some international institutions, and not pursuing its use as an international means of payment. The use of the dollar as a means of payment increases the demands for U.S. financial services. Giving up this role would be costly for the U.S. economy and therefore is likely to face resistance from the U.S. Congress. It is hence more politically feasible to pursue changes in the reserve asset role of the dollar, which are also in the long-term interest of the U.S. given the gradual erosion of confidence in the dollar as a reserve currency.

Developing Countries Interests

The developing countries that hold large-scale dollar reserves would incur fewer costs from the depreciation of the dollar if they transform a large part of their reserves into SDRs through a substitution account. If the dollar depreciates in the subsequent years, it will be essential to determine who bears the cost. Under a cost-sharing mechanism, the depositors of large dollar reserves would equally share the potential costs with the United States, but as shown previously, the creation of a counterpart account could actually balance the substitution account without any costs to any parties involved. In the absence of this counterpart account, however, the developing countries with large dollar reserves would partly bear the cost of holding the substitution account solvent. Yet, these additional costs would still be less than the losses of holding dollar reserves in case of its depreciation. Thus, in the short run, it is in the best interest of developing countries to switch a large part of their reserves into SDRs.

In the medium run, periodic SDR allocations of the IMF would give the developing countries the benefit of sharing in the seigniorage resulting from reserve creation. If they continue to rely on other reserve currencies, the seigniorage benefits would be captured by the issuers of these currencies, i.e. the United States and Eurozone countries. Thus, the policy of SDR allocations is the only way that developing countries would receive part of the seigniorage benefits. Coupled with the potential costs of rising instability from shifting to a multi-currency system and the costs of an ongoing global imbalance from relying on the dollar as the major reserve currency, the advantages of moving towards an SDR-centred system for the developing countries are obvious. It should also be emphasized that the cost of borrowing reserve currencies from the international markets is rather large for many developing countries, and this would come down to very low levels if the IMF allocates SDRs to its members regularly.

These benefits in the medium run would extend over the long run for developing countries whose currencies have no potential to become a reserve currency. For the obvious country whose currency is a candidate to become a major reserve currency in the future, i.e. China, some argued that the long-run benefit of the ability to finance a larger current account deficit and expand domestic consumption significantly due to the demand for renminbi as a reserve currency might exceed the benefit of an SDR-based system (Subramanian, 2009). There are, however, good reasons to resist assuming the role of the reserve currency: 1) there are disadvantages of becoming a large short-term debtor due to potential instabilities this situation creates;2) there are costs of the instability of a multi-currency system as the central banks lose from speculation about the best reserve currency composition with the greatest yield; and 3) the creditor countries receive leverage over debtor countries, having the potential to restrict their policy autonomy (Williamson, 2009). Given these potential disadvantages and costs, the benefits from running a larger deficit do not necessarily result in net benefits overall. Even if attaining the reserve currency status for the renminbi is the goal over the long term, the transition from the dollar to the SDR would carry net advantages for China in the short and medium runs.

An SDR-based reform of the reserve system would also bring to the developing countries the additional benefit of financing global public goods such as green technology transfers and health initiatives. The enhanced funding opportunities may help developing countries achieve MDGs.

Complementary Reforms for the SDR-Based System

Several supplementary reforms are necessary for the SDR-based reserve system to function better than the current system. These include the International Clearance Unit that was originally proposed by Keynes and the regional financial arrangements including reserve pools such as the Chiang Mai Initiative, the Latin American Reserve Fund, and the Arab Monetary Fund.

International Clearance Unit and the IMF's Role

Counter-cyclical IMF allocations of SDRs and IMF lending to countries with SDRs are essential as central mechanisms to prevent any inflationary bias new SDR allocations might generate. It should be recognized, however, that the current conditionalities of the IMF credit lines and the associated negative public opinion require a complementary reform. As Ocampo suggested, it is time to create "an overdraft facility that can be used unconditionally by all IMF members up to a certain limit and for a pre-established time" (2010b, p. 15). An international clearance unit as an overdraft facility was part of Keynes' original plan but was never adopted due to disagreements among major powers. The importance of this facility is that it would partly overcome the asymmetric adjustment between surplus and deficit countries, which would not be eliminated by the shift to the SDR as a reserve currency. A penalty can be introduced for accumulating large surpluses or excessive reserves by suspending the right to receive SDR allocations (Ocampo 2010b, p. 16). A more ambitious quota reform is required to make sure not only that the new SDR allocations are distributed more evenly, but also that the decision-making within the IMF becomes more democratic, representing the realities of the current world economy.

Regional Arrangements

The Stiglitz Commission (2009) proposed that the new global reserve system should be built in a bottom-up fashion where the agreements among regional monetary arrangements play a central role. This proposal conceives the future of the IMF as a network of regional reserve funds, which is similar to the design of the World Bank coexisting with many regional development banks and other sub-regional institutions. Regional arrangements would play an important role in improving the global macroeconomic stability through a number of mechanisms: 1) by enhancing collective insurance through additional forms of credit lines and swaps, 2) by providing a venue for macroeconomic policy coordination and dialogue, and 3) by increasing the voice of smaller countries to which they respond in a timely fashion (Ocampo, 2006).

Reserve pools, among other forms of regional monetary arrangements (such as swap lines, common central banks, and payments agreements), have been major institutions that provided additional forms of collective insurance to their members. The most successful of the reserve pools are:

The Chiang Mai Initiative (CMI):

Launched in May 2000 in Chiang Mai, Thailand, the CMI consists of ten member countries of the Association of Southeast Asian Nations (ASEAN) and China, Japan, and South Korea. Its central objective was to offer short-term financial support for neighboring countries that run into balance of payments problems. Originally consisting only of swap agreements among ASEAN+3 countries, the CMI was multilateralized since May 2009. That is, the bilateral currency swap agreements were transformed into a single regional pooling arrangement (Volz et al., 2011). In the wake of the financial crisis in 2009, the funds of the CMI were raised to US$120 billion. The funding available to potential borrowers is relatively small compared to the region's foreign exchange reserves. However, it is still a multiple of the quotas of the region's less developed countries at the IMF. One downside to the operations of CMI is the "IMF link", which allows only 20% of the credit lines to be used if the borrowing country does not have a lending program with the IMF (Volz et al. 2011). This provision certainly limits the scope of lending although the size of the lending pool is substantially large.

The Latin American Reserve Fund (FLAR):

Founded in 1978 by the Andean countries (Bolivia, Colombia, Ecuador, Peru, and Venezuela), the FLAR enlarged in 1989 when Costa Rica joined and in 2008 when Uruguay joined. The initial objective was to give short-term liquidity support to the balance of payments of its members. Currently, it pursues additional goals of "improving the liquidity of international reserve investments; facilitating the restructuring of public debt; and helping to harmonize the member countries' monetary, exchange and financial policies" (Volz, 2011). Despite its smaller size relative to CMI (US$1.77 billion), the Fund provides privileged access to smaller and less developed countries such as Bolivia and Ecuador, which can borrow up to 350% of their capital contribution while others only up to 250%. The heterogeneity of member countries assures that their demand for liquidity does not coincide in time, indicating that the Fund has good capacity to prevent the spread of contagion in the region.

The Arab Monetary Fund (AMF):

Founded in 1976 by 22 Middle Eastern countries, the AMF provides a balance of payments support similar to the CMI and the FLAR. Besides, it promotes Arab monetary cooperation by supporting the development of Arab financial markets and the regulatory mechanisms that would support the effective functioning of these markets. Furthermore, it offers advice to member states about the investment of financial resources into foreign markets, and it encourages intra-regional trade. The total amount of capital contributions to the Fund was US$2.8 billion in 2009. The potential borrowers are net energy importers, and in this sense, the Fund can be thought of providing short-term lending from the world's largest gas and oil producers to the importers of energy in the Middle East in order to support their balance of payments. Although there is no formal IMF link, the borrowing countries that apply for extensive funding are implicitly expected to apply to international lending institutions.

Overall, despite their limitations in terms of mostly being a supplement to the IMF lending, these regional reserve funds provide a collective mechanism to defend individual countries from any speculative attacks on their currencies. Therefore, they should be seen as complementary lending facilities with crucial stabilizing functions.

The argument is that it is possible to overcome the technical and political difficulties in launching an SDR- based reserve system and a fully SDR-funded IMF to build a more stable and equitable international monetary system. Under this system, the IMF would allocate SDRs counter-cyclically and treat them as deposits of countries, which could be used in lending to them. This would be valid even though SDRs are confined to act as a means of payment only among central banks and not private agents. Reforming the system in this way would be effective in addressing some of the core imperfections of the current global monetary system. Developing countries, in particular, would benefit from this reform given that they would receive part of the seigniorage related to global monetary creation, and that their balance of payments needs require them to use their SDR allocations more frequently.

Previous estimates of SDR allocations point to a range of US$200-300 billion a year as a conservative estimate. The estimate in this paper is based on the annual average of world demand for additional reserves with the lower bound US$246 billion over 2000-05 and the upper bound US$443 billion over 2006-10. Thus, the recent recommendation of Stiglitz et al. (2011) for annual allocations ranging from US$240-400 billion is a reasonable estimate to satisfy the rapidly rising world demand for reserves. The most recent Fund proposal falls short of this amount with a range of US$117-133 billion a year for three years beginning in 2014.

One of the most important technical difficulties in the transition towards an SDR-based reserve system is the costs of a substitution account which are deficiency payments that might arise from a decline in US interest rate, an increase in SDR interest rate, or a depreciation of the US dollar. In the 1970s negotiations, the United States refused to take responsibility as the single country to maintain the dollar value of SDR-denominated assets in the account, which brought the negotiations to a dead end. To prevent such an outcome again, one should pay attention to two aspects of the substitution account. First, historical simulations indicate that the substitution account alternates between periods of surplus and deficit in terms of dollars, and the deficiency payments arise only in periods of deficit. To avoid the accumulation of deficits, a counterpart account - which would be credited when the substitution account is in surplus and debited when it is in deficit - should be established. This would effectively eliminate the problem of which country would pay for the potential costs.

Second, in the absence of a counterpart account, different cost-sharing mechanisms could be devised by:

(i) dividing the cost (the sum of deficiency payments) between the United States and the IMF as the latter can use its dollar or gold holdings; (ii) distributing the costs among depositor countries proportional to their shares of dollar deposits in the account such that larger holders pay a higher cost; (iii) having the IMF collect an annual fee of 1 percent of the dollar reserves deposited in the account such that depositors pay for the costs and establish a fund to invest these fees in US government securities; and (iv) modifying the previous option to have this fund and the United States share the cost in some way.

The historical simulations indicate that even in the worst-case scenario when all downside risks take place, the costs of maintaining the solvency of the substitution account would be 0.2 percent of total US foreign assets and 0.3 percent of US GDP in 2008, which is negligible and it would even be much smaller if there is a cost-sharing mechanism in which the US pays half or less than half of the cost depending on the arrangement. Other technical questions discussed could be summed up in four points. First, would the new SDR allocations have an inflationary effect? The answer is no as long as they are not made in times of strong global demand and inflationary concerns and the central banks sterilize any undesired money creation. Second, could other currencies be added into the SDR basket to better represent the composition of world output and lower the volatility of the value of SDR? The answer is positive for renminbi which satisfies IMF's criteria by being issued by one of the largest exporters and by being freely usable for payments, settlements of trade, and some FDI investments as long as the central bank guarantees its convertibility in official transactions.

Third, what would be the role of SDR-denominated bonds in this reform agenda? These bonds have many advantages for developing countries by not only being a substitute for the other major short-term assets but also serving as a means to push further quota reforms at the IMF. The SDR-denominated bonds could replace other global assets if they reach sufficient market depth and liquidity with the involvement of private investors. Fourth, is the absence of private markets a problem for the use of SDRs as a central bank asset in reserve accumulation or for intervening in the foreign exchange markets? The answer is no because as long as central banks accept SDRs from one another in exchange for convertible currencies, the SDR is a medium of exchange in inter-central bank transactions. For intervening in the foreign exchange markets, each IMF member has to guarantee the obligation to freely accept SDRs in exchange for their currencies.

Political difficulties result from a diversion of interests between the United States (and other reserve issuers), and the developing countries as demanders of reserves. In the initial stages of reform, it is important to promote the SDRs only as a reserve asset and not as an international means of payment, which would be costly for the US economy. This would make the reform more politically feasible. This is also in the long-term interest of the U.S. given the gradual erosion of confidence in the dollar as a reserve currency and the risk of losing monetary policy autonomy. For the developing countries holding dollar reserves, the costs of transition to an SDR-based system would be lower than the cost of dollar depreciation if they exchange their reserves for SDRs through a substitution account. In the medium run, new SDR allocations would allow developing countries to share in the seigniorage resulting from reserve creation and lower the cost of borrowing international reserves. Converting the unutilized SDRs of industrial countries into the equity of global funds would help finance global public goods including climate change mitigation and adaptation and global health initiatives. By and large, the reserve issuers and demanders have more interests in common than in opposition to lay the building blocks of an SDR- based international monetary system that relies on a network of the IMF and regional monetary arrangements.

History Of The Federal Reserve

1775-1791: U.S. Currency

To finance the American Revolution, the Continental Congress printed the new nation's first paper money. Known as "continentals," the fiat money notes were issued in such quantity they led to inflation, which, though mild at first, rapidly accelerated as the war progressed. Eventually, people lost faith in the notes, and the phrase "Not worth a continental" came to mean "utterly worthless."

1791-1811: First Attempt at Central Banking

At the urging of then-Treasury Secretary Alexander Hamilton, Congress established the First Bank of the United States, headquartered in Philadelphia, in 1791. It was the largest corporation in the country and was dominated by big banking and money interests. Many agrarian-minded Americans uncomfortable with the idea of a large and powerful bank opposed it. When the bank's 20-year charter expired in 1811 Congress refused to renew it by one vote.

1816-1836: A Second Try Fails

By 1816, the political climate was once again inclined toward the idea of a central bank; by a narrow margin, Congress agreed to charter the Second Bank of the United States. But when Andrew Jackson, a central bank foe, was elected president in 1828, he vowed to kill it. His attack on its banker-controlled power touched a popular nerve with Americans, and when the Second Bank's charter expired in 1836, it was not renewed.

1836-1865: The Free Banking Era

State-chartered banks and unchartered "free banks" took hold during this period, issuing their own notes, redeemable in gold or species. Banks also began offering demand deposits to enhance commerce. In response to a rising volume of check transactions, the New York Clearinghouse Association was established in 1853 to provide a way for the city's banks to exchange checks and settle accounts.

1863: National Banking Act

During the Civil War, the National Banking Act of 1863 was passed, providing for nationally chartered banks, whose circulating notes had to be backed by U.S. government securities. An amendment to the act required taxation on state bank notes but not national bank notes, effectively creating a uniform currency for the nation. Despite taxation on their notes, state banks continued to flourish due to the growing popularity of demand deposits, which had taken hold during the Free Banking Era.

1873-1907: Financial Panics Prevail

Although the National Banking Act of 1863 established some measure of currency stability for the growing nation, bank runs and financial panics continued to plague the economy. In 1893, a banking panic triggered the worst depression the United States had ever seen, and the economy stabilized only after the intervention of financial mogul J.P. Morgan. It was clear that the nation's banking and financial system needed serious attention.

1907: A Very Bad Year

In 1907, speculation on Wall Street failed, triggering a particularly severe banking panic. J.P. Morgan was again called upon to avert disaster. By this time, most Americans were calling for reform of the banking system, but the structure of that reform was cause for deep division among the country's citizens. Conservatives and powerful "money trusts" in the big eastern cities were vehemently opposed by "progressives." But there was a growing consensus among all Americans that a central banking authority was needed to ensure a healthy banking system and provide for an elastic currency.

1908-1912: The Stage is Set for Decentralized Central Bank

The Aldrich-Vreeland Act of 1908, passed as an immediate response to the panic of 1907, provided for emergency currency issues during crises. It also established the National Monetary Commission to search for a long-term solution to the nation's banking and financial problems. Under the leadership of Senator Nelson Aldrich, the commission developed a banker-controlled plan. William Jennings Bryan and other progressives fiercely attacked the plan; they wanted a central bank under public, not banker, control. The 1912 election of Democrat Woodrow Wilson killed the Republican Aldrich plan, but the stage was set for the emergence of a decentralized central bank.

1912: Woodrow Wilson as Financial Reformer

Though not personally knowledgeable about banking and financial issues, Woodrow Wilson solicited expert advice from Virginia Representative Carter Glass, soon to become the chairman of the House Committee on Banking and Finance, and from the Committee's expert advisor, H. Parker Willis, formerly a professor of economics at Washington and Lee University. Throughout most of 1912, Glass and Willis labored over a central bank proposal, and by December 1912, they presented Wilson with what would become, with some modifications, the Federal Reserve Act.

1913: The Federal Reserve System is Born

From December 1912 to December 1913, the Glass- Willis proposal was hotly debated, molded, and reshaped. By December 23, 1913, when President Woodrow Wilson signed the Federal Reserve Act into law, it stood as a classic example of compromise—a decentralized central bank that balanced the competing interests of private banks and populist sentiment.

1914: Open for Business

Before the new central bank could begin operations, the Reserve Bank Operating Committee, comprised of Treasury Secretary William McAdoo, Secretary of Agriculture David Houston, and Comptroller of the Currency John Skelton Williams, had the arduous task of building a working institution around the bare bones of the new law. But, by November 16, 1914, the 12 cities chosen as sites for regional Reserve Banks were open for business, just as hostilities in Europe erupted into World War I.

1914-1919: Fed Policy During the War

When World War I broke out in mid-1914, U.S. banks continued to operate normally, thanks to the emergency currency issued under the Aldrich- Vreeland Act of 1908. But the greater impact in the United States came from the Reserve Banks' ability to discount bankers' acceptances. Through this mechanism, the United States aided the flow of trade goods to Europe, indirectly helping to finance the war until 1917, when the United States officially declared war on Germany, and financing our own war effort became paramount.

The 1920s: The Beginning of Open Market Operations

Following World War I, Benjamin Strong, head of the New York Fed from 1914 to his death in 1928, recognized that gold no longer served as the central factor in controlling credit. Strong's aggressive action to stem a recession in 1923 through a large purchase of government securities gave clear evidence of the power of open market operations to influence the availability of credit in the banking system. During the 1920s, the Fed began using open market operations as a monetary policy tool. During his tenure, Strong also elevated the stature of the Fed by promoting relations with other central banks, especially the Bank of England.

1929-1933: The Market Crash and the Great Depression

During the 1920s, Virginia Representative Carter Glass warned that stock market speculation would lead to dire consequences. In October 1929, his predictions seemed to be realized when the stock market crashed, and the nation fell into the worst depression in its history. From 1930 to 1933, nearly 10,000 banks failed, and by March 1933, newly inaugurated President Franklin Delano Roosevelt declared a bank holiday, while government officials grappled with ways to remedy the nation's economic woes. Many people blamed the Fed for failing to stem speculative lending that led to the crash, and some also argued that inadequate understanding of monetary economics kept the Fed from pursuing policies that could have lessened the depth of the Depression.

1933: The Depression Aftermath

In reaction to the Great Depression, Congress passed the Banking Act of 1933, better known as the Glass- Steagall Act, calling for the separation of commercial and investment banking and requiring the use of government securities as collateral for Federal Reserve notes. The Act also established the Federal Deposit Insurance Corporation (FDIC), placed open market operations under the Fed, and required bank holding companies to be examined by the Fed, a practice that was to have profound future implications, as holding companies became a prevalent structure for banks over time. Also, as part of the massive reforms taking place, Roosevelt recalled all gold and silver certificates, effectively ending the gold and any other metallic standard.

1935: More Changes to Come

The Banking Act of 1935 called for further changes in the Fed's structure, including the creation of the Federal Open Market Committee (FOMC) as a separate legal entity, removal of the Treasury Secretary and the Comptroller of the Currency from the Fed's governing board and establishment of the members' terms at 14 years. Following World War II, the Employment Act added the goal of promising maximum employment to the list of the Fed's responsibilities. In 1956 the Bank Holding Company Act named the Fed as the regulator of bank holding companies owning more than one bank, and in 1978 the Humphrey-Hawkins Act required the Fed chairman to report to Congress twice annually on monetary policy goals and objectives.

1951: The Treasury Accord

The Federal Reserve System formally committed to maintaining a low-interest rate peg on government bonds in 1942 after the United States entered World War II. It did so at the request of the Treasury to allow the federal government to engage in cheaper debt financing of the war. To maintain the pegged rate, the Fed was forced to give up control of the size of its portfolio as well as the money stock. The conflict between the Treasury and the Fed came to the fore when the Treasury directed the central bank to maintain the peg after the start of the Korean War in 1950.

President Harry Truman and Secretary of the Treasury John Snyder were both strong supporters of the low-interest rate peg. The President felt that it was his duty to protect patriotic citizens by not lowering the value of the bonds that they had purchased during the war. Unlike Truman and Snyder, the Federal Reserve was focused on the need to contain inflationary pressures in the economy caused by the intensification of the Korean War. Many on the Board of Governors, including Marriner Eccles, understood that the forced obligation to maintain the low peg on interest rates produced an excessive monetary expansion that caused inflation. After a fierce debate between the Fed and the Treasury for control over interest rates and U.S. monetary policy, their dispute was settled resulting in an agreement known as the Treasury-Fed Accord. This eliminated the obligation of the Fed to monetize the debt of the Treasury at a fixed rate and became essential to the independence of central banking and how monetary policy is pursued by the Federal Reserve today.

The 1970s-1980s: Inflation and Deflation

The 1970s saw inflation skyrocket as producer and consumer prices rose, oil prices soared and the federal deficit more than doubled. By August 1979, when Paul Volcker was sworn in as Fed chairman, drastic action was needed to break inflation's stranglehold on the U.S. economy. Volcker's leadership as Fed chairman during the 1980s, though painful in the short term, was successful overall in bringing double-digit inflation under control.

1980 Setting the Stage for Financial Modernization

The Monetary Control Act of 1980 required the Fed to price its financial services competitively against private sector providers and to establish reserve requirements for all eligible financial institutions. The act marks the beginning of a period of modern banking industry reforms. Following its passage, interstate banking proliferated, and banks began offering interest-paying accounts and instruments to attract customers from brokerage firms. Barriers to insurance activities, however, proved more difficult to circumvent. Nonetheless, momentum for change was steady, and by 1999 the Gramm-Leach-Bliley Act was passed, in essence, overturning the Glass-Steagall Act of 1933 and allowing banks to offer a menu of financial services, including investment banking and insurance.

The 1990s: The Longest Economic Expansion

Two months after Alan Greenspan took office as the Fed chairman, the stock market crashed on October 19, 1987. In response, he ordered the Fed to issue a one-sentence statement before the start of trading on October 20: "The Federal Reserve, consistent with its responsibilities as the nation's central bank, affirmed today its readiness to serve as a source of liquidity to support the economic and financial system." The 10- year economic expansion of the 1990s came to a close in March 2001 and was followed by a short, shallow recession ending in November 2001. In response to the bursting of the 1990s stock market bubble in the early years of the decade, the Fed lowered interest rates rapidly. Throughout the 1990s, the Fed used monetary policy on a number of occasions including the credit crunch of the early 1990s and the Russian default on government securities to keep potential financial problems from adversely affecting the real economy. The decade was marked by generally declining inflation and the longest peacetime economic expansion in our country's history.

September 11, 2001

The effectiveness of the Federal Reserve as a central bank was put to the test on September 11, 2001, as the terrorist attacks on New York, Washington, and Pennsylvania disrupted U.S. financial markets. The Fed issued a short statement reminiscent of its announcement in 1987: "The Federal Reserve System is open and operating. The discount window is available to meet liquidity needs." In the days that followed, the Fed lowered interest rates and loaned more than $45 billion to financial institutions to provide stability to the U.S. economy. By the end of September, Fed lending had returned to pre- September 11 levels and a potential liquidity crunch had been averted. The Fed played a pivotal role in dampening the effects of the September 11 attacks on U.S. financial markets.

January 2003: Discount Window Operation Changes In 2003, the Federal Reserve changed its discount window operations to have rates at the window set above the prevailing Fed Funds rate and provide rationing of loans to banks through interest rates.

2006 and Beyond: Financial Crisis and Response During the early 2000s

During the early 2000s, low mortgage rates and expanded access to credit made homeownership possible for more people, increasing the demand for housing and driving up house prices. The housing boom got a boost from increased securitization of mortgages—a process in which mortgages were bundled together into securities that were traded in financial markets. Securitization of riskier mortgages expanded rapidly, including subprime mortgages made to borrowers with poor credit records. House prices faltered in early 2006 and then started a steep slide, along with home sales and construction. Falling house prices meant that some homeowners owed more on their mortgages than their homes were worth. Starting with subprime mortgages, more and more homeowners fell behind on their payments. Eventually, this spread to prime mortgages as well. The rising number of delinquencies on subprime mortgages was a wake-up call to lenders and investors that many residential mortgages were not nearly as safe as once believed. As the mortgage meltdown intensified, the magnitude of expected losses rose dramatically. Because millions of U.S. mortgages were repackaged as securities, losses spread across the globe. It became very difficult to determine the value of many loans and mortgage-related securities. In addition, the widespread use of complex and exotic financial instruments made it even harder to figure out the vulnerability of financial institutions to losses. Institutions became increasingly reluctant to lend to each other.

The situation reached a crisis point in 2007 when these fears about the financial health of other firms led to massive disruptions in the wholesale bank lending market. As a result, rates on short-term loans rose sharply relative to the overnight federal funds rate. In the fall of 2008, two large financial institutions failed: the investment bank Lehman Brothers and the savings and loan Washington Mutual. The extensive web of connections among major financial institutions meant that the failure of one could start a cascade of losses throughout the financial system, threatening many other institutions. Confidence in the financial sector collapsed and stock prices of financial institutions around the world plummeted. Banks were unable to sell most types of loans to investors because securitization markets had stopped working. As a result, banks and investors clamped down on many types of loans by tightening standards and demanding higher interest rates—a classic credit crunch. Tight credit weakened spending on big-ticket items financed by borrowing: houses, cars, and business investment. The hit to household wealth was another factor causing people to cut back on spending as they struggled to rebuild depleted savings. With demand weakening, businesses canceled expansion plans and laid-off workers. The U.S. economy entered a recession, a period in which the level of economic activity was shrinking, in December 2007. The recession had been relatively mild until the fall of 2008 when financial panic intensified, causing job losses to soar.

As short-term markets froze, the Federal Reserve expanded its own collateralized lending to financial institutions to ensure that they had access to the critical funding needed for day-to-day operations. In March 2008, the Federal Reserve created two programs to provide short-term secured loans to primary dealers similar to discount-window loans provided to banks. Conditions in these markets improved considerably in 2009. The possible failure of the investment bank Bear Stearns early in 2008 carried the risk of a domino effect that would have severely disrupted financial markets. To contain the damage, the Federal Reserve provided non-recourse loans to the bank JP Morgan

Chase to facilitate its purchase of certain Bear Stearns assets. Following the collapse of the investment bank Lehman Brothers, financial panic threatened to spread to several other key financial institutions, potentially leading to a cascade of failures and a meltdown of the global financial system. The Federal Reserve provided secured loans to the giant insurance company American International Group (AIG) because of its central role in guaranteeing financial instruments.

In normal times, banks borrow from each other for terms ranging from overnight to several months. Starting in August 2007, banks became increasingly reluctant to make short-term loans to each other. In response, the Federal Reserve increased the availability of one- and three-month discount-window loans to banks through the creation of the Term Auction Facility. It also created swap lines with foreign central banks to increase the availability of dollar-denominated loans to banks in other countries. In the spring of 2009, the Federal Reserve, in conjunction with other federal regulatory agencies, conducted an exhaustive and unprecedented review of the financial condition of the 19 largest U.S. banks. This included a "stress test" that measured how well these banks could weather a bad economy over the next two years. Banks that didn't have enough of a capital cushion to protect them from loan losses under the most adverse economic scenario were required to raise new money from the private sector or accept federal government funds from the Troubled Asset Relief Program.

In response to the economic crisis, the Federal Reserve's policy-making body, the Federal Open Market Committee, slashed its target for the federal funds rate over more than a year, bringing it nearly to zero by December 2008. This is the lowest level for federal funds in over 50 years and effectively is as low as this key rate can go. Cutting the federal funds rate helped lower the cost of borrowing for households and businesses on mortgages and other loans. To stimulate the economy and further lower borrowing costs, the Federal Reserve turned to unconventional policy tools. It purchased $300 billion in longer-term Treasury securities, which are used as benchmarks for a variety of longer-term interest rates, such as corporate bonds and fixed-rate mortgages. To support the housing market, the Federal Reserve authorized the purchase of $1.25 trillion in mortgage-backed securities guaranteed by agencies such as Freddie Mac and Fannie Mae and about $175 billion of mortgage agency longer-term debt. These Federal Reserve purchases have reduced mortgage interest rates, making home purchases more affordable.

Federal Reserve Board (FRB)
What Is the Federal Reserve Board (FRB)?

The Board of Governors of the Federal Reserve System, also known as the Federal Reserve Board (FRB), is the governing body of the Federal Reserve System. The FRB was established by the Banking Act of 1935. The members are statutorily tasked with giving a "fair representation of the financial, agricultural, industrial, and commercial interests and geographical divisions of the country.

How the Federal Reserve Board (FRB) Works

The Board of Governors of the Federal Reserve System called the Federal Reserve Board or FRB for short, is a seven-member body that governs the Federal Reserve System, the U.S. central bank in charge of making the country's monetary policy.

The FRB is considered an independent agency of the federal government. The Fed has a statutory mandate to maximum employment and stable prices at moderate long-term interest rates, and the FRB chair and other officials frequently testify before Congress, but it makes monetary policy independently of the legislative or executive branches and is structured like a private corporation.

Appointments, Terms, and Roles

The president appoints the FRB's members, and they are confirmed by the Senate. Each is appointed to a single 14-year term but may serve shorter or longer periods. A new board member serves the remainder of the outgoing member's term if any. The new member may then be reappointed to one full term. If a replacement has not been confirmed when that term expires, they may continue to serve, so that a member can serve for much longer than 14 years. However, the President is allowed to remove a member from the board, given sufficient cause. Terms are staggered so that a new one begins every two years. Once appointed, each board member operates independently.

The chair and vice-chair for the supervision of the Federal Reserve Board are appointed to four-year terms by the president from among the board's existing members. They can be reappointed to these leadership roles as many times as their term limits as board members allow.

The board of governors includes several subcommittees with their chairs and vice-chairs. These are the committees on board affairs; consumer and community affairs; economic and financial monitoring and research; financial stability; Federal Reserve Bank affairs; supervision and regulation; payments, clearing, and settlement; and the subcommittee on smaller regional and community banking.

Current Federal Reserve Board
Jerome H. Powell (Chair)
Richard H. Clarida (Vice Chair)
Randal K. Quarles (Vice Chair for Supervision)
Michelle W. Bowman
Lael Brainard Christopher Waller

Duties of the Federal Reserve Board (FRB)

The Federal Reserve Board members' most important role is as members of the Federal Open Market Committee (FOMC), which is in charge of the open market operations that determine the federal funds rate, one of the global economy's most important benchmarks interest rates. In addition to the seven governors, the FOMC consists of the president of the Federal Reserve Bank of New York and a rotating set of four other branch presidents. The chair of the FRB also chairs the FOMC.

The FRB is directly in charge of two other monetary policy tools, the discount rate (based on suggestions from the regional branches) and reserve requirements. It is also tasked with supervising the Fed's 12 regional branches.

Federal Open Market Committee (FOMC)

What Is the Federal Open Market Committee (FOMC)?

The Federal Open Market Committee (FOMC) is the branch of the Federal Reserve System (FRS) that determines the direction of monetary policy specifically by directing open market operations (OMOs). The committee is made up of 12 members: the seven members of the Board of Governors; the president of the Federal Reserve Bank of New York; and four of the remaining 11 Reserve Bank presidents on a rotating basis.

When it is reported in the news that the Fed has changed interest rates, it is the result of the FOMC's regular meetings.

Understanding the Federal Open Market Committee (FOMC)

The 12 members of the FOMC meet eight times a year to discuss whether there should be any changes to near-term monetary policy.1 A vote to change policy would result in either buying or selling U.S. government securities on the open market to promote the growth of the national economy.

Members of the committee are typically categorized as hawks favoring tighter monetary policies, doves who favor stimulus, or centrists/moderates who are somewhere in between. Traditionally, the chair of the FOMC is also the chair of the Board of Governors. The current chair of the Federal Reserve Board is Jerome Powell, who was sworn in on Feb. 5, 2018, and is serving a four-year term. Powell is considered a moderate. Other members include Richard Clarida, Randal Quarles, Lael Brainard, Michelle Bowman, and Christopher Waller. The remaining position is vacant as of July 26, 2021 The vice-chair of the FOMC is also the president of the Federal Reserve Bank of New York,2 a position currently filled by John C. Williams, who took office on June 18, 2018, as the 11th president and chief executive officer of the Second District, Federal Reserve Bank of New York. The president of the Federal Reserve Bank of New York serves continuously, while the presidents of the other Reserve Banks serve one-year terms on a three-year rotating schedule (except for Cleveland and Chicago, which rotate on a two-year basis).

The one-year rotating seats of the FOMC are always comprised of one Reserve Bank president from each of the following groups:

Boston, Philadelphia, and Richmond
Cleveland and Chicago
St. Louis, Dallas, and Atlanta
Kansas City, Minneapolis, and San Francisco
The geographic-group system helps ensure that all
regions of the United States receive fair representation.

Current FOMC Members

Name Position
Jerome H. Powell Chair of the Federal Reserve Board (FOMC Chair)
John C. Williams President of the New York Federal Reserve Bank (FOMC Vice-Chair)
Michelle W. Bowman Member of Federal Reserve Board
Lael Brainard Member of Federal Reserve Board
Richard H. Clarida Vice Chair of Federal Reserve Board
Thomas I. Barkin President of the Federal Reserve Bank of Richmond
Raphael W. Bostic President of the Federal Reserve Bank of Atlanta
Mary C. Daly President of the Federal Reserve Bank of San Francisco
Charles L. Evans President of the Federal Reserve Bank of Chicago
Randal K. Quarles Vice Chair of Supervision of Federal Reserve Board
Christopher J. Waller Member of Federal Reserve Board
Currently Empty Member of Federal Reserve Board

FOMC Meetings

The Federal Open Market Committee (FOMC) has eight regularly scheduled meetings each year, but they can meet more often if the need should arise.1 The meetings are not held in public and are therefore the subject of much speculation on Wall Street, as analysts attempt to predict whether the Fed will tighten or loosen the money supply with a resulting increase or decrease in interest rates. In recent years, FOMC meeting minutes have been made public following the meetings.

During the meeting, members discuss developments in the local and global financial markets, as well as economic and financial forecasts. All participants—the Board of Governors and all 12 Reserve Bank presidents—share their views on the country's economic stance and converse on the monetary policy that would be most beneficial for the country. After much deliberation by all participants, only designated FOMC members to get to vote on a policy that they consider appropriate for the period.

FOMC Operations

Through OMOs, adjusting the discount rate, and setting bank reserve requirements, the Federal Reserve possesses the tools necessary to increase or decrease the money supply. The Fed's Board of Governors is in charge of setting the discount rate and reserve requirements, while the FOMC is specifically in charge of OMOs, which entails buying and selling government securities. For example, to tighten the money supply and decrease the amount of money available in the banking system, the Fed would offer government securities for sale.

Securities bought by the FOMC are deposited in the Fed's System Open Market Account (SOMA), which consists of a domestic and a foreign portfolio. The domestic portfolio holds U.S. Treasuries and federal agency securities, while the foreign portfolio holds investments denominated in euros and Japanese yen.8

The FOMC can hold these securities until maturity or sell them when they see fit, as granted by the Federal Reserve Act of 1913 and Monetary Control Act of 1980. A percentage of the Fed's SOMA holdings are held in each of the 12 regional Reserve Banks. However, the Federal Reserve Bank of New York executes all of the Fed's open market transactions.

Simply put, the process begins with the results of the meeting being communicated to the SOMA manager, who relays them to the trading desk at the Federal Reserve Bank of New York, which then conducts transactions of government securities on the open market until the FOMC mandate is met.

The interaction of all of the Fed's policy tools determines the federal funds rate or the rate at which depository institutions lend their balances at the Federal Reserve to each other on an overnight basis. The federal funds rate, in turn, directly influences other short-term rates and indirectly influences long-term interest rates; foreign exchange rates, and the supply of credit and demand for investment, employment, and economic output.

Example of FOMC Policy

On Jan. 29, 2019, at its annual organizational meeting, the FOMC unanimously reaffirmed its "Statement of Longer-Run Goals and Monetary Policy Strategy" with an updated reference to the median of participants' estimates of the longer-run normal rate of unemployment in its "Summary of Economic Projections" (December 2018).

This statement is based on the FOMC's commitment to fulfilling a statutory mandate from Congress to promote maximum employment, stable prices, and moderate long-term interest rates. Because monetary policy determines the inflation rate over the long term, the FOMC can specify a longer-run goal for inflation. In the statement, the FOMC reaffirmed its analysis that a 2% target inflation rate was the rate most consistent with its statutory mandate.

Why Is The Federal Reserve Independent?

Many people are surprised to learn that the central bank of the United States, the Federal Reserve, operates for the most part independently of the government. The combined public and private structure of the Federal Reserve (Fed) is highly controversial, especially in the aftermath of the financial crisis of 2007-2008.

The role of the Fed as the central bank in the U.S. and its position of influence highlights the question of whether or not central banks should be independent of the political nature of government.

The Fed as Quasi-Governmental

The monetary decisions of the Federal Reserve do not have to be ratified by the President (or anyone else in the Executive Branch). The Fed receives no funding from Congress and the members of the Board of Governors, who are appointed, serve 14-year terms. These terms do not coincide with presidential terms, creating further independence.

However, the Federal Reserve is subject to oversight by Congress, which aims to ensure it achieves the economic objectives of maximum employment and stable prices. And the Fed Chair must submit a semi¬annual report on monetary policy to Congress.

Why Be Independent?

The primary justification for an independent Federal Reserve is the need to insulate it from short-term political pressures. Without a degree of autonomy, the Fed could be influenced by election-focused politicians into enacting an excessively expansionary monetary policy to lower unemployment in the short term. This could lead to high inflation and failure to control unemployment over the long term.

Indeed, proponents of central bank independence argue that political pressure is too great to let it interfere with monetary policy and macroeconomic decision-making. In particular, politicians have short-term goals of re-election, which tend to favor inflationary policies that give the illusion of boosting wages and employment, but at the expense of longer-term growth.

Furthermore, inflation can undermine the purchasing power of currency and harm creditors and savers.

Advocates of autonomy thus argue that an independent Fed will better address long-term economic objectives. Independence can also make it easier to execute policies that are politically unpopular but serve a greater public interest. Another argument is that the central bank should be filled with economists and other experts, rather than politicians or those under political sway.

Arguments Against Independence

Critics argue that it is unconstitutional for Congress to assign monetary power to an independent quasi-governmental agency. According to the Constitution, Congress has the power to coin money and regulate its value. In 1913, Congress delegated this power to the Fed through the 1913 Federal Reserve Act. However, some argue that such a delegation is fundamentally unconstitutional. Opponents of Fed independence also suggest that it is undemocratic to have an unelected agency, unaccountable to the US public, dictating monetary policy.

Another argument against independence is that it fosters poor coordination between the fiscal policy put in place by congress (i.e. taxation and spending) and the monetary policy enacted by central banks. For instance, if the government is cutting taxes (loose fiscal policy), but the central bank is raising interest rates (tight monetary policy), creating a mismatch that undermines both's efforts.

What Do The Federal Reserve Banks Do?

In 1913, the Federal Reserve Act established the Federal Reserve System (FRS), an independent governmental entity that would serve as a central bank to the U.S. government. In addition, to the board of governors, the board of directors, and the Federal Open Market Committee (FOMC), the act formed 12 Federal Reserve Banks spread out across the United States.

Together, the banks' mission is to provide the nation with a stable monetary policy and a safe and flexible financial system, but what do the Reserve Banks do?

A Network of Regional Fed Banks

The 12 Reserve Banks oversee the regional member banks, protect regional economic interests, and ensure that the public has clout in central bank decisions. Although Federal Reserve Banks don't operate for profit, they generate income from interest on government securities acquired through Fed monetary policy actions and financial services provided to depository institutions. Each year, after accounting for operational expenses, the regional banks return any excess earnings to the U.S. Treasury. Overall, these regional banks are involved with four general tasks: formulate monetary policy, supervise financial institutions, facilitate government policy, and provide payment services.

Facilitating Monetary Policy

Regional banks enforce the monetary policies that the Board of Directors sets by ensuring that all depository institutions—commercial and mutual savings banks, savings and loan associations, and credit unions—can access cash at the current discount rate.

They also assist the FOMC and the Federal Reserve by contributing to the formulation of monetary policy. Each regional bank has a staff of researchers that collects information about its region, analyzes economic data, and investigates developments in the economy. These researchers advise regional bank presidents on policy matters who then publicize the information to their constituencies in order to survey public opinion.

Supervising Member Institutions

The Board of Governors delegates most supervisory responsibilities over member institutions to the Reserve Banks, which are charged with conducting on-site and off-site examinations, inspecting state-chartered banks and authorizing banks to become chartered. They also ensure that depository institutions maintain the proper reserve ratio—the requirement outlining the proportion of deposits that must be held on reserve as cash. In addition, Reserve Banks are responsible for writing regulations for consumer credit laws and ensuring that communities have access to sufficient credit from banks.

Servicing the Government

Reserve Banks also engage in financial services to the federal government by acting as the liaison between the Department of Treasury and depository institutions. The regional banks collect unemployment and income tax, excise taxes to deposit to the Treasury, and issue and redeem bonds as well as T-bills in the specified allotments to retain the desired level of bank reserves.

Additionally, Reserve Banks maintain the Treasury Department's transaction and operating accounts by holding collateral for government agencies to secure funds currently on deposit with private institutions. The banks also make regular interest payments on outstanding government obligations.

Servicing Depository Institutions

Distributing paper money to chartered depository institutions is another one of the Reserve Banks' duties. Excess cash is deposited at the Reserve Banks when demand is light; when demand is heavy, institutions can withdraw or borrow from the banks. The regional banks have the electronic infrastructure in place to handle wire transfers, moving funds between its 7,800 depository institutions.

In addition, the Reserve Banks are a check-clearing system that processes 18 billion checks annually and routes them to the correct depository institution. The Reserve Banks also provide automated clearinghouses that allow depository institutions to exchange payment to carry out payroll direct deposits and mortgage payments.

Often called a bank for banks, the network of Reserve Banks carries out the orders of the Fed, provides support for member banks around the country and cultivates safe banking practices. Many of the services provided by these banks are similar to the services that ordinary banks offer, except the Reserve Banks provide these services to banks rather than individuals or business customers. Reserve Banks hold cash reserves and make loans to depository institutions, circulate currency, and provide payment services to thousands of banks.

Without these regional banks, the Federal Reserve wouldn't be able to sanction its policies across the nation, govern the thousands of depository institutions, or ensure that the central bank hears the voices of people from each region when making policy judgments. They are the fiscal agents and the operating arms of the central bank.

Understanding the Federal Reserve Balance Sheet

The Federal Reserve System is the central bank of the United States and is responsible for the nation's monetary policy. The Fed's primary goals are to promote maximum employment, stable prices, and manage long-term interest rates. The Fed also helps to create stability in the financial system, especially during times of recession—or negative economic growth—and financial instability.

The Fed uses various programs and initiatives to accomplish its goals, and the result usually leads to a change in the composition of the Fed's balance sheet. The Fed can increase or decrease the amount and scope of assets or liabilities on its balance sheet, which in turn, increases or decreases the money supply within the economy. However, some critics argue the Fed has gone too far and tried to do too much in response to recessions and crises.

The Balance Sheet of the Federal Reserve Bank

Just like any other balance sheet, the Fed's balance sheet consists of assets and liabilities. Each week, the Fed issues its H.4.1 report, which provides a consolidated statement of the condition of all the Federal Reserve banks, in terms of their assets and liabilities.

For decades, the Fed watchers have relied on movements in assets or liabilities of the Fed to predict changes in economic cycles. The financial crisis of 2007-08 not only made the Fed's balance sheet more complex but also aroused the interest of the general public.4 Before going into the details, it would be better to take a look at the Fed's assets first and then its liabilities.

For much of its history, the Fed's balance sheet was actually quite a sleepy topic. Issued every Thursday, the weekly balance sheet report (or H.4.1) includes items that might seem at first glance typical of most company balance sheets. It lists all assets and liabilities, providing a consolidated statement of the condition of all 12 regional Federal Reserve Banks.

The Fed's assets consist primarily of government securities and the loans it extends to its regional banks. Its liabilities include U.S. currency in circulation. Other liabilities include money held in the reserve accounts of member banks and U.S. depository institutions.

The weekly balance sheet report became popular in the media during the financial crisis starting in 2007. When launching their quantitative easing in response to the ongoing financial crisis, the Fed's balance sheet gave analysts an idea of the scope and scale of Fed market operations at the time. In particular, the Fed's balance sheet allowed analysts to see details surrounding the implementation of an expansionary monetary policy used during the 2007-2009 crisis.

The Fed's Assets

The essence of the Fed's balance sheet is similar to any other balance sheet since anything for which the Fed has to pay money becomes the Fed's asset. In other words, if the Fed were to hypothetically buy bonds or stocks by paying newly issued money for them, those investments would become assets.

Treasury Securities

Traditionally, the Fed's assets have mainly consisted of government securities, such as U.S. Treasuries and other debt instruments. More than 60% or nearly $5 trillion of the $7.69 trillion in assets include various types of U.S. Treasuries as of March 17, 2021. The Treasury securities include Treasury notes, which have maturity dates that range from two to 10 years, and Treasury bills, or T-bills, which have short-term maturities such as four, eight, 13, 26, and 52 weeks.

Mortgage-backed Securities

The other significant amount of assets on the Fed's balance sheet include mortgage-backed securities, which are investments that are made up of a basket of home loans. These fixed-income securities are packaged and sold to investors by banks and financial institutions. The Fed owns more than $2 trillion in mortgage-backed securities on its balance sheet as of March 17, 2021.

Loans

The assets also include loans extended to member banks through the repo and discount window.6 The Fed's discount window is a lending facility for commercial banks other depository institutions. The Fed charges an interest rate—called the federal discount rate—to banks for borrowing from the Fed's discount window.

When the Fed buys government securities or extends loans through its discount window, it simply pays by crediting the reserve account of the member banks through an accounting or book entry. In case member banks wish to convert their reserve balances into hard cash, the Fed provides them with dollar bills.

Thus, for the Fed, assets include securities it has purchased through open market operations (OMO), as well as any loans extended to banks which will be repaid at a later time. Open market operations refer to when the Fed buys and sells securities in the market, which are usually U.S. Treasury securities. Whether the Fed buys or sells securities, the central bank influences the money supply in the U.S. economy.

The Fed's Liabilities

One of the interesting things about the Fed's liabilities is that currency in circulation, like the green dollar bills in your pocket, are reflected as liabilities. Apart from this, the money lying in the reserve account of member banks and U.S. depository institutions also forms a part of the Feds' liabilities. As long as the dollar bills lie with the Fed, they would be treated as neither assets nor liabilities.

The dollar bills become the Fed's liabilities only when the Fed puts them in circulation by purchasing assets. Of the nearly $7.65 trillion in liabilities as of March 17, 2021, the Fed has just over $2 trillion as currency notes and $5.3 trillion in deposits on its balance sheet.

The size of different components of the Fed liabilities keeps on changing. For instance, if the member banks wish to convert the money lying in their reserve accounts into hard cash, the value of the currency in circulation would increase, and the credit balance in reserve accounts would decrease. But overall, the size of the Fed's liabilities increases or decreases whenever the Fed buys or sells its assets.

The Fed also requires commercial banks to hold on to a certain minimum amount of deposits, known as reserves. The reserve ratio is the portion of reservable liabilities that commercial banks must hold onto rather than lend out or invest and is currently set at 0% effective March 26, 2020.9 As this is an asset for commercial banks, it is reciprocally a liability for the central bank.

The Meaning of Liability

The Fed can very well discharge its existing liabilities by creating additional liabilities. For instance, if you take your $100 bill to the Fed, it can very well pay you back in five 20-dollar bills or any other combination you like. The Fed can't, in any manner, be compelled to discharge its liabilities in terms of any other tangible goods or services. At best, you could receive government securities by paying back in dollars whenever the Fed is selling.

Beyond this, the Fed's liabilities are only as good as something written on a piece of paper. In a nutshell, paper promises beget only other kinds of paper promises.

The Fed's Balance Sheet Expansion

Theoretically, there is no limit up to which the Fed can expand its balance sheet. The balance sheet of the Fed automatically expands when the Fed buys assets. Likewise, the Fed's balance sheet automatically contracts when it sells them.

However, the contraction of a balance sheet differs from expansion in the sense that there is a limit beyond which the Fed can't contract its balance sheet. That limit is determined by the value of assets. Unlike dollar bills, which can be used for buying assets, the Fed can't create government securities out of thin air. It can't sell more government securities that it owns.

Apart from this, while expanding or contracting its own balance sheet, the Fed has to also take into account its effect on the economy. Generally, the Fed buys assets as a part of its monetary policy action whenever it intends to increase the money supply for keeping the interest rates closer to the Federal funds rate, and sells assets when it intends to decrease the money supply.10

Quantitative easing (QE) is an unconventional monetary policy in which a central bank purchases government securities or other securities from the market to lower interest rates and increase the money supply. Using the Fed's balance sheet through quantitative easing remains somewhat controversial. Although these efforts certainly helped ease the bank sector's liquidity issues during the financial crisis, critics contend QE was a giant drawback and was a distortion of free-market principles. Today, markets are still sorting out the short-term bump but longer-term side effects of the government stepping in.

The Fed's Programs

Sometimes the Fed has to take steps out of its normal course, as it did during the 2007-08 financial crisis and the response to the coronavirus pandemic.

Financial Crisis of 2007-2008

During the height of the financial crisis, the Fed's balance sheet ballooned with toxic assets having different kinds of acronyms. The Fed had assets worth $870 billion on its books toward the end of August 2007, just before the start of the financial crisis, and the same stood at $2.23 trillion at the end of 2009.

So we have seen Term Auction Facility (TAF), Primary Dealer Credit Facility (PDCF), and many other complex acronyms reflected as the Fed's assets over a period.11 12 Some argued that the Fed intervention in this manner helped in putting markets back on track.

Coronavirus Pandemic of 2020 and 2021

In response to the economic hardship facing the United States due to the coronavirus pandemic, the Fed took several steps to stabilize and support the banking system, corporations, and small businesses.

The Fed's stimulus actions were carried out through multiple lending facilities, including the Paycheck Protection Program Liquidity Facility (PPPLF), which provided money to financial institutions so that they could lend that money to small businesses. The Main Street Lending Program was another lending program that helped to provide loans to small and mid-sized companies, but the program ended on January 8, 2021.

The Fed also directly purchased existing investment-grade corporate bonds of U.S. companies—called the Secondary Market Corporate Credit Facility (SMCCF). In addition to corporate bonds, the Fed also bought exchange-traded funds (ETFs)that contained bonds.

The Fed's purchases created an enormous demand for corporate debt, allowing companies to issue new bonds to raise capital or money. All of these actions increased the Fed's balance sheet from $4.7 trillion on March 17, 2020, to over $7.6 trillion by March 17, 2021.

Reserve Requirements

What Are Reserve Requirements?

Reserve requirements are the amount of cash that banks must have, in their vaults or at the closest Federal Reserve bank, in line with deposits made by their customers. Set by the Fed's board of governors, reserve requirements are one of the three main tools of monetary policy—the other two tools are open market operations and the discount rate.

On March 15, 2020, the Federal Reserve Board announced that reserve requirements ratios would be set to 0%, effective March 26, 2020. Before the change, effective March 26, 2020, the reserve requirement ratios on net transactions accounts differed based on the number of net transaction accounts at the institution.

Basics of Reserve Requirements

Banks loan funds to customers based on a fraction of the cash they have on hand. The government makes one requirement of them in exchange for this ability: keep a certain amount of deposits on hand to cover possible withdrawals. This amount is called the reserve requirement, and it is the rate that banks must keep in reserve and are not allowed to lend.

The Federal Reserve's Board of Governors sets the requirement as well as the interest rate banks get paid on excess reserves. The Financial Services Regulatory Relief Act of 2006 gave the Federal Reserve the right to pay interest on excess reserves. The effective date on which banks started getting paid interest was Oct. 1, 2008.2 This rate of interest is referred to as the interest rate on excess reserves and serves as a proxy for the federal funds rate.

The reserve requirement is another tool that the Fed has at its disposal to control liquidity in the financial system. By reducing the reserve requirement, the Fed is executing an expansionary monetary policy, and conversely, when it raises the requirement, it's exercising a contractionary monetary policy. This action cuts liquidity and causes a cooldown in the economy.

Reserve Requirements History

The practice of holding reserves started with the first commercial banks during the early 19th century. Each bank had its own note that was only used within its geographic area of operation. Exchanging it to another banknote in a different region was expensive and risky because of the lack of information about funds at the other bank.

To overcome this problem, banks in New York and New Jersey arranged for voluntary redemption at each other's branches on the condition that the issuing bank and redeeming bank both maintained an agreed-upon deposit of gold or its equivalent. Subsequently, the National Bank Act of 1863 imposed 25% reserve requirements for banks under its charge.3 Those requirements and a tax on state banknotes in 1865 ensured that national bank notes replaced other currencies as a medium of exchange.

The creation of the Federal Reserve and its constituent banks in 1913 as a lender of last resort further eliminated risks and costs required in maintaining reserves and pared-down reserve requirements from their earlier high levels.4 For example, reserve requirements for three types of banks under the Federal Reserve were set at 13%, 10%, and 7% in 1917.5

In response to the COVID-19 pandemic, the Federal Reserve reduced the reserve requirement ratio to zero across all deposit tiers, effective March 26, 2020.6 this reduction aimed to jump-start the economy by allowing banks to use additional liquidity to lend to individuals and businesses.

Reserve Requirements vs. Capital Requirements

Some countries don't have reserve requirements. These countries include Canada, the United Kingdom, New Zealand, Australia, Sweden, and Hong Kong. Money can't be created without limit, but instead, some of these countries must adhere to capital requirements, which is the amount of capital a bank or financial institution must hold as required by its financial regulator.

Reserve Requirement Example

As an example, assume a bank had $200 million in deposits and is required to hold 10%. The bank is now allowed to lend out $180 million, which drastically increases bank credit. In addition to providing a buffer against bank runs and a layer of liquidity, reserve requirements are also used as a monetary tool by the Federal Reserve. By increasing the reserve requirement, the Federal Reserve is essentially taking money out of the money supply and increasing the cost of credit. Lowering the reserve requirement pumps money into the economy by giving banks excess reserves, which promotes the expansion of bank credit and lowers rates.

Reserve Ratio Definition What Is the Reserve Ratio?

The reserve ratio is the portion of reservable liabilities that commercial banks must hold onto, rather than lend out or invest. This is a requirement determined by the country's central bank, which in the United States is the Federal Reserve. It is also known as the cash reserve ratio.

The minimum amount of reserves that a bank must hold on to is referred to as the reserve requirement and is sometimes used synonymously with the reserve ratio. The reserve ratio is specified by the Federal Reserve Board's Regulation D. Regulation D created a set of uniform reserve requirements for all depository institutions with transaction accounts, and requires banks to provide regular reports to the Federal Reserve.

The Formula for the Reserve Ratio

Reserve Requirement=DepositsxReserve Ratio

As a simplistic example, assume the Federal Reserve determined the reserve ratio to be 11%. This means if a bank has deposits of $1 billion, it is required to have $110 million on reserve ($1 billion x .11 = $110 million). During the pandemic of 2020, the Federal Reserve reduced the reserve requirement to 0%.

What Does the Reserve Ratio Tell You?

The Federal Reserve uses the reserve ratio as one of its key monetary policy tools. The Fed may choose to lower the reserve ratio to increase the money supply in the economy. A lower reserve ratio requirement gives banks more money to lend, at lower interest rates, which makes borrowing more attractive to customers.

Conversely, the Fed increases the reserve ratio requirement to reduce the amount of funds banks have to lend. The Fed uses this mechanism to reduce the supply of money in the economy and control inflation by slowing the economy down.

The Fed also sets reserve ratios to ensure that banks have money on hand to prevent them from running out of cash in the event of panicked depositors wanting to make mass withdrawals. If a bank doesn't have the funds to meet its reserve, it can borrow funds from the Fed to satisfy the requirement.

Banks must hold reserves either as cash in their vaults or as deposits with a Federal Reserve Bank. On Oct. 1, 2008, the Federal Reserve began paying interest to banks on these reserves.2 This rate is referred to as the interest rate on required reserves (IORR). There is also an interest rate on excess reserves (IOER), which is paid on any funds bank deposits with the Federal Reserve more than their reserve requirement.

U.S. commercial banks are required to hold reserves against their total reservable liabilities (deposits) which cannot be lent out by the bank. Reservable liabilities include net transaction accounts, nonpersonal time deposits, and Eurocurrency liabilities.

Reserve Ratio Guidelines

The Board of Governors of the Federal Reserve has the sole authority over changes in reserve requirements within limits specified by law. As of March 26, 2020, the reserve requirement was set at 0%.1 That's when the board eliminated the reserve requirement due to the global financial crisis. This means that banks aren't required to keep deposits at their Reserve Bank. Instead, they can use the funds to lend to their customers.

The last time the Fed updated its reserve requirements for different depository institutions before the pandemic was in January 2019. Banks with more than $124.2 million in net transaction accounts were required to maintain a reserve of 10% of net transaction accounts. Banks with more than $16.3 million to $124.2 million needed to reserve 3% of net transaction accounts. Banks with net transaction accounts of up to $16.3 million or less were not required to have a reserve requirement. The majority of banks in the United States fell into the first category. The Fed set a 0% requirement for nonpersonal time deposits and Eurocurrency liabilities.

Reserve Ratio and the Money Multiplier

In fractional reserve banking, the reserve ratio is key to understanding how much credit money banks can make by lending out deposits. For example, if a bank has $500 million in deposits, it must hold $50 million, or 10%, in reserve. It may then lend out the remaining 90%, or $450 million, which will make its way back to the banking system as new deposits. Banks may then lend out 90% of that amount, or $405 million while retaining $45 million in reserves. That $405 million will be deposited again, and so on. Ultimately, that $500 million in deposits can turn into $5 billion in loans, where the 10% reserve requirement defines the so-called money multiplier

How Interest Rate Cuts Affect Consumers

The Federal Reserve's open market committee (FOMC) meets regularly to decide what, if anything, to do with short-term interest rates. Indeed, interest rates are closely watched by analysts and economists as these key figures play out in every asset market around the globe. Do stock traders almost always rejoice when the Fed cuts interest rates but does a rate cut equal good news for everyone? Rate cuts tend to favor borrowers, but hurt lenders and savers.

But what about ordinary households? Interest rate changes also have large impacts on consumer behavior and the level of consumption an economy can expect. This is because higher rates translate to larger borrowing and financing costs for things purchased on credit. Read on to find out exactly where this comes into play.

What Are Interest Rates?

When the Fed "cuts rates," this refers to a decision by the FOMC to reduce the federal fund's target rate. The target rate is a guideline for the actual rate that banks charge each other on overnight reserve loans. Rates on interbank loans are negotiated by the individual banks and, usually, stay close to the target rate.

The target rate may also be referred to as the "federal funds rate" or the "nominal rate."

The federal funds rate is important because many other rates, domestic and international, are linked directly to it or move closely with it.

Why Do Rates Change?

The federal funds rate is a monetary policy tool used to achieve the Fed's goals of price stability (low inflation) and sustainable economic growth. Changing the federal funds rate influences the money supply, beginning with banks and eventually trickling down to consumers.

The Fed lowers interest rates to stimulate economic growth. Lower financing costs can encourage borrowing and investing. However, when rates are too low, they can spur excessive growth and perhaps inflation. Inflation eats away at purchasing power and could undermine the sustainability of the desired economic expansion.

On the other hand, when there is too much growth, the Fed will raise interest rates. Rate increases are used to slow inflation and return growth to more sustainable levels. Rates cannot get too high, because more expensive financing could lead the economy into a period of slow growth or even contraction.

On August 27, 2020, the Federal Reserve announced that it will no longer raise interest rates due to unemployment falling below a certain level of inflation remains low. It also changed its inflation target to an average, meaning that it will allow inflation to rise somewhat above its 2% target to make up for periods when it was below 2%.2

Financing

The Fed's target rate is the basis for bank-to-bank lending. The rate banks charge their most creditworthy corporate customers is known as the prime lending rate. Often referred to as "the prime," this rate is linked directly to the Federal Reserve's target rate. Prime is pegged at 300 basis points (3%) above the target rate.

Consumers can expect to pay prime plus a premium depending on factors such as their assets, liabilities, income, and creditworthiness.

A rate cut could help consumers save money by reducing interest payments on certain types of financing that are linked to prime or other rates, which tend to move in tandem with the Fed's target rate.

Mortgages

A rate cut can prove beneficial with home financing, but the impact depends on what type of mortgage the consumer has, whether fixed or adjustable and which rate the mortgage is linked to.

For fixed-rate mortgages, a rate cut will have no impact on the amount of the monthly payment. Low rates can be good for potential homeowners, but fixed-rate mortgages do not move directly with the Fed's rate changes. A Fed rate cut changes the short-term lending rate, but most fixed-rate mortgages are based on long-term rates, which do not fluctuate as much as short-term rates.

Generally speaking, when the Fed issues a rate cut, adjustable-rate mortgage (ARM) payments will decrease. The amount by which a mortgage payment changes will depend on the rate the mortgage uses when it resets. Many ARMs are linked to short-term Treasury yields, which tend to move with the Fed, or the London Interbank Offered Rate (LIBOR), which does not always move with the Fed. Many home-equity loans and home-equity lines of credit (HELOCs) are also linked to prime or LIBOR.

Credit Cards

The impact of a rate cut on credit card debt also depends on whether the credit card carries a fixed or variable rate. For consumers with fixed-rate credit cards, a rate cut usually results in no change. Many credit cards with variable rates are linked to the prime rate, so a federal funds rate cut will typically lead to lower interest charges.

It is important to remember that even if a credit card carries a fixed rate, credit card companies can change interest rates whenever they want to, as long as they provide advanced notice (check your terms for the required notice).

Savings Accounts

When the Fed cuts interest rates, consumers usually earn less interest on their savings. Banks will typically lower rates paid on cash held in bank certificates of deposits (CDs), money market accounts, and regular savings accounts. The rate cut usually takes a few weeks to be reflected in bank rates.

CDs and Money Market Accounts

If you have already purchased a bank CD, there is no need to worry about a rate cut because your rate is locked in. But if you plan to purchase additional CDs, a rate cut will result in new, lower rates.

Deposits placed into money market accounts (MMAs) will see similar activity. Banks use MMA deposits to invest in traditionally safe assets like CDs and Treasury bills, so a Fed rate cut will result in lower rates for money market account holders.

Money Market Funds

Unlike a money market account, a money market fund (MMF) is an investment account. While both pay higher rates than regular savings accounts, they may not have the same response to a rate cut.

The response of MMF rates to a rate cut by the Fed depends on whether the fund is taxable or tax-free (like one that invests in municipal bonds). Taxable funds usually adjust in line with the Fed, so in the event of a rate cut, consumers can expect to see lower rates offered by these securities.

Because of their tax-exempt status, rates on municipal money market funds already fall beneath their taxable counterparts and may not necessarily follow the Fed. These funds also may be linked to different rates, such as LIBOR or the Security Industry and Financial Markets Association (SIFMA) Municipal Swap Index.

Investments

If you have a 401(k) plan or a brokerage account, interest rates also directly impact your investment portfolio. Lower rates often are a boost to stocks (except, perhaps to financial sector stocks) but at the same time are a drag on bond prices. Lower rates also let investors with margin accounts take greater advantage of leverage at lower rates, increasing their effective purchasing power.

On the other hand, higher rates can pull stocks lower but increase the value of bonds. In general, longer-term bonds are more sensitive to interest rate changes than near-term bonds.

How Moves in the Fed Funds Rate Affect the US Dollar Changes in the federal funds rate can impact the U.S. dollar. When the Federal Reserve increases the federal funds rate, it typically increases interest rates throughout the economy. The higher yields attract investment capital from investors abroad seeking higher returns on bonds and interest-rate products. Global investors sell their investments denominated in their local currencies in exchange for U.S. dollar-denominated investments. The result is a stronger exchange rate in favor of the U.S. dollar.

Understanding the Fed Funds Rate

The federal funds rate is the rate banks charge each other for lending their excess reserves or cash. Some banks have excess cash, while other banks might have short-term liquidity needs. The fed funds rate is a target rate set by the Federal Reserve Bank and is usually the basis for the rate that commercial banks lend to each other.

However, the fed funds rate has a far more sweeping impact on the economy as a whole. The fed funds rate is a key tenet of interest rate markets and is used to set the prime rate, which is the rate banks charge their clients for loans. Also, mortgage and loan rates, as well as deposit rates for savings, are impacted by any changes in the fed funds rate.

The Fed, through the FOMC or Federal Open Market Committee, adjusts rates depending on the economy's needs. If the FOMC believes the economy is growing too quickly, and inflation or rising prices might likely occur, the FOMC will increase the fed funds rate.

Conversely, if the FOMC believes that the economy is struggling or might dip into a recession, the FOMC would lower the fed funds rate. Higher rates tend to slow lending and the economy, while lower rates tend to spur lending and economic growth.

The Fed's mandate is to use monetary policy to help achieve maximum employment and stable prices. During the financial crisis of 2008 and the Great Recession, the Fed held the federal funds rate at or near 0% to 0.25%. In the following years, the Fed increased rates as the economy improved.

Inflation, the Fed Funds, and the Dollar

One of the ways the Fed achieves full employment and stable prices is by setting its inflation target rate at 2%. In 2011, the Fed officially adopted a 2% annual increase in the price index for personal consumption expenditures as its target.

In other words, as the inflation component of the index rises, it signals that the prices of goods are rising in the economy. If prices are rising, but wages aren't growing, people's purchasing power is declining. Inflation also impacts investors. For example, if an investor is holding a fixed-rate bond paying 3% and inflation rises to 2%, the investor is only earning 1% in real terms.

When the economy is weak, inflation falls since there's less demand for goods to push up prices. Conversely, when the economy is strong, rising wages increase spending, which can spur higher prices. Keeping inflation at a growth rate of 2% helps the economy grow at a steady pace and allows wages to naturally rise.

Adjustments to the federal funds rate can also affect inflation in the United States. When the Fed increases interest rates, it encourages people to save more and spend less, reducing inflationary pressures. Conversely, when the economy is in a recession or growing too slowly, and the Fed reduces interest rates, it stimulates spending spurring inflation.

How the Dollar Helps the Fed with Inflation

Of course, many other factors impact inflation besides the Fed and have resulted in the inflation rate remaining below the Fed's 2% target for years. The U.S. dollar exchange rate plays a role in inflation.

For example, as U.S. exports are sold to Europe, buyers need to convert euros to dollars to make the purchases. If the dollar is strengthening, the higher exchange rate causes Europeans to pay more for U.S. goods, based solely on the exchange rate. As a result, U.S. export sales may decline if the dollar is too strong.

Also, a strong dollar makes imports cheaper. If U.S. companies are buying goods from Europe in euros and the euro is weak, or the dollar is strong, those imports are cheaper. The result is cheaper products at U.S. stores, and those lower prices translate to low inflation.

Cheap imports help keep inflation low since U.S. companies that produce goods domestically have to keep their prices low to compete with cheap imports. A stronger dollar aids in making imports cheaper and acts as a natural hedge for reducing inflation risk in the economy.

As you can imagine, the Fed monitors inflation closely along with the level of strength of the dollar before making any decisions regarding the fed funds rate.

Example of the Fed Funds and the U.S. Dollar

- Below we can see the fed funds rate since the mid-1990s; the gray areas denote recessions:
- In the mid-1990s, the fed funds rate rose from 3% to eventually over 6%.
- The fed funds rate was lowered in 2001 to 1% from over 6% a year earlier.
- In the mid-2000s, the fed funds rate was hiked with an improving economy.
- In 2008, the fed funds rate was lowered again from over 5% to nearly zero and stayed at zero for several years.
- The Federal Funds Rates above were retrieved from FRED or the Federal Reserve Bank of St. Louis.

As the fed funds rate increases, overall rates in the economy rise. If global capital flows are moving into dollar-denominated assets, chasing higher rates of return, the dollar strengthens.

In the mid-1990s, when the fed hiked rates, the dollar rose as measured by the dollar index, which measures the exchange rates of a basket of currencies.

In 2002 when the Fed cut rates, the dollar weakened dramatically.

The dollar correlation to the fed funds broke down somewhat in the mid-2000s. As the economy grew and rates rose, the dollar didn't follow suit.

The dollar began to rebound only to fall again in 2008 and 2009.

As the economy emerged from the Great Recession, the dollar fluctuated for years.

Against the backdrop of a stronger economy and eventual Fed hikes, the dollar began to rise again from 2014 to 2018.

Open Market Operations (OMO)
What Are Open Market Operations (OMO)?

Open market operations (OMO) refers to the Federal Reserve (Fed) practice of buying and selling primarily U.S. Treasury securities on the open market to regulate the supply of money that is on reserve in U.S. banks. This supply is what's available to loan out to businesses and consumers. It purchases Treasury securities to increase the supply of money and sells them to reduce the supply of money.

Understanding Open Market Operations

The objective of OMOs is to manipulate the short-term interest rate and the supply of base money in an economy.1By conducting open market operations, the Federal Reserve can achieve the desired target federal funds rate by providing or removing liquidity to commercial banks by buying or selling government bonds with them.

Basically, open market operations are the tools the Fed uses to reach that target rate by buying and selling securities in the open market. The central bank can increase the money supply and lower the market interest rate by purchasing securities using newly created money. Similarly, the central bank can sell securities from its balance sheet and take money out of circulation, putting positive pressure on interest rates.

The Federal Open Market Committee (FOMC) is the entity that carries the Federal Reserve's OMO policy. The Board of Governors of the Federal Reserve sets a target federal funds rate and then the FOMC implements the open market operations that achieve that rate. The federal funds rate is the interest percentage that banks charge each other for overnight loans. This constant flow of vast sums of money allows banks to keep their cash reserves high enough to meet the demands of customers while putting excess cash to use.

The federal funds rate also is a benchmark for other rates, influencing the direction of everything from savings deposit rates to home mortgage rates and credit card interest. The Federal Reserve sets a target federal funds rate to keep the U.S. economy on an even keel and to forestall the ill effects of uncontrolled price inflation or deflation.

U.S. Treasuries are government bonds that are purchased by many individual consumers as a safe investment. They are also traded on the money markets and are purchased and held in large quantities by financial institutions and brokerages.

Open market operations allow the Federal Reserve to buy or sell Treasuries in such large quantities that it has an impact on the supply of money distributed in banks and other financial institutions around the U.S.

Permanent open market operations (POMO) refers to when a central bank constantly uses the open market to buy and sell securities to adjust the money supply. It has been one of the tools used by the Federal Reserve to implement monetary policy and influence the American economy. Permanent open market operations (POMOs) are the opposite of temporary open market operations, which are used to add or drain reserves available to the banking system temporarily, thereby influencing the federal funds rate.

The federal funds rate is a benchmark that influences all other interest rates for everything from home mortgages to savings deposits.

Up or Down?

There are only two ways Treasury rates can move, and that's up or down. In the Federal Reserve's language, the policy is expansionary or contractionary.

If the Fed's goal is expansionary, it buys Treasuries in order to pour cash into the banks. That puts pressure on the banks to lend that money out to consumers and businesses. As the banks compete for customers, interest rates drift downwards.

Consumers are able to borrow more to buy more. Businesses are eager to borrow more to expand.

If the Fed's goal is contractionary, it sells Treasuries to pull money out of the system. Money gets tight, and interest rates drift upwards. Consumers pull back on their spending. Businesses trim their growth plans, and the economy slows down.

Frequently Asked Questions

Why Does the Federal Reserve Conduct Open Market Operations?

Basically, open market operations are the tools the Federal Reserve (Fed) uses to achieve the desired target federal funds rate by buying and selling, mainly, U.S. Treasuries in the open market. The central bank can increase the money supply and lower the market interest rate by purchasing securities using newly created money. Similarly, the central bank can sell securities from its balance sheet and take money out of circulation, thereby pressuring market interest rates to rise.

What Are Permanent Open Market Operations (POMO)?

Permanent open market operations (POMO) refers to a central bank practice of constantly using the open market to buy and sell securities to adjust the money supply. It has been one of the tools used by the Federal Reserve to implement monetary policy and influence the American economy. POMOs are the opposite of temporary open market operations, which are used to add or drain reserves available to the banking system temporarily, thereby influencing the federal funds rate.

How Does the Federal Funds Rate Affect Banks?

By law, commercial banks must maintain a reserve equal to a certain percentage of their deposits in an account at a Federal Reserve bank. Any money in their reserve that exceeds the required level is available for lending to other banks that might have a shortfall. The interest rate the lending bank can charge is the federal funds rate, or fed funds rate.

Tight Monetary Policy
What Is a Tight Monetary Policy?

Tight, or contractionary monetary policy is a course of action undertaken by a central bank such as the Federal Reserve to slow down overheated economic growth, to constrict spending in an economy that is seen to be accelerating too quickly, or to curb inflation when it is rising too fast.

The central bank tightens policy or makes money tight by raising short-term interest rates through policy changes to the discount rate, also known as the federal funds rate. Boosting interest rates increases the cost of borrowing and effectively reduces its attractiveness. Tight monetary policy can also be implemented via selling assets on the central bank's balance sheet to the market through open market operations (OMO).

Understanding Tight Monetary Policy

Central banks around the world use monetary policy to regulate specific factors within the economy. Central banks most often use the federal funds rate as a leading tool for regulating market factors.

The federal funds rate is used as a base rate throughout global economies. It refers to the rate at which banks lend to each other and is also known as the discount rate. An increase in the federal funds rate is followed by increases in the borrowing rates throughout the economy.

Rate increases make borrowing less attractive as interest payments increase. It affects all types of borrowing including personal loans, mortgages, and interest rates on credit cards. An increase in rates also makes saving more attractive, as savings rates also increase in an environment with a tightening policy. The Fed may also raise reserve requirements for member banks, in a bid to shrink the money supply or perform open-market operations, by selling assets like U.S. Treasuries, to large investors. This large number of sales lowers the market price of such assets and increases their yields, making it more economical for savers and bondholders.

On August 27, 2020, the Federal Reserve announced that it will no longer raise interest rates due to unemployment falling below a certain level of inflation remains low. It also changed its inflation target to an average, meaning that it will allow inflation to rise somewhat above its 2% target to make up for periods when it was below 2%.

Tight monetary policy is different from—but can be coordinated with—a tight fiscal policy, which is enacted by legislative bodies and includes raising taxes or decreasing government spending. When the Fed lowers rates and makes the environment easier to borrow, it is called monetary easing.

A Benefit of Tight Monetary Policy: Open Market Treasury Sales

In a tightening policy environment, the Fed can also sell Treasuries on the open market in order to absorb some extra capital during a tightened monetary policy environment. This effectively takes capital out of the open markets as the Fed takes in funds from the sale with the promise of paying the amount back with interest.

Tightening policy occurs when central banks raise the federal funds rate, and easing occurs when central banks lower the federal funds rate.

In a tightening monetary policy environment, a reduction in the money supply is a factor that can significantly help to slow or keep the domestic currency from inflation. The Fed often looks at tightening monetary policy during times of strong economic growth.

An easing monetary policy environment serves the opposite purpose. In an easing policy environment, the central bank lowers rates to stimulate growth in the economy. Lower rates lead consumers to borrow more, also effectively increasing the money supply.

Many global economies have lowered their federal fund's rates to zero, and some global economies are in negative rate environments. Both zero and negative-rate environments benefit the economy through easier borrowing. In an extreme negative rate environment, borrowers even receive interest payments, which can create a significant demand for credit.

Expansionary Policy

What Is an Expansionary Policy?

The expansionary, or loose policy is a form of macroeconomic policy that seeks to encourage economic growth. The expansionary policy can consist of either monetary policy or fiscal policy (or a combination of the two). It is part of the general policy prescription of Keynesian economics, to be used during economic slowdowns and recessions in order to moderate the downside of economic cycles.

Understanding Expansionary Policy

The basic objective of expansionary policy is to boost aggregate demand to make up for shortfalls in private demand. It is based on the ideas of Keynesian economics, particularly the idea that the main cause of recessions is a deficiency in aggregate demand. Expansionary policy is intended to boost business investment and consumer spending by injecting money into the economy either through direct government deficit spending or increased lending to businesses and consumers.

From a fiscal policy perspective, the government enacts expansionary policies through budgeting tools that provide people with more money. Increasing spending and cutting taxes to produce budget deficits means that the government is putting more money into the economy than it is taking out. Expansionary fiscal policy includes tax cuts, transfer payments, rebates, and increased government spending on projects such as infrastructure improvements.

For example, it can increase discretionary government spending, infusing the economy with more money through government contracts. Additionally, it can cut taxes and leave a greater amount of money in the hands of the people who then go on to spend and invest.

Expansionary monetary policy works by expanding the money supply faster than usual or lowering short-term interest rates. It is enacted by central banks and comes about through open market operations, reserve requirements, and setting interest rates. The U.S. Federal Reserve employs expansionary policies whenever it lowers the benchmark federal funds rate or discount rate, decreases required reserves for banks, or buys Treasury bonds on the open market. Quantitative Easing, or QE, is another form of expansionary monetary policy.

On August 27, 2020, the Federal Reserve announced that it will no longer raise interest rates due to unemployment falling below a certain level of inflation remains low. It also changed its inflation target to an average, meaning that it will allow inflation to rise somewhat above its 2% target to make up for periods when it was below 2%.

For example, when the benchmark federal funds rate is lowered, the cost of borrowing from the central bank decreases, giving banks greater access to cash that can be lent in the market. When reserve requirements decline, it allows banks to lend a higher proportion of their capital to consumers and businesses. When the central bank purchases debt instruments, it injects capital directly into the economy.

The Risks of Expansionary Monetary Policy

Expansionary policy is a popular tool for managing low-growth periods in the business cycle, but it also comes with risks. These risks include macroeconomic, microeconomic, and political economy issues.

Gauging when to engage in expansionary policy, how much to do, and when to stop requires sophisticated analysis and involves substantial uncertainties. Expanding too much can cause side effects such as high inflation or an overheated economy. There is also a time lag between when a policy move is made and when it works its way through the economy.

This makes up-to-the-minute analysis nearly impossible, even for the most seasoned economists. Prudent central bankers and legislators must know when to halt money supply growth or even reverse course and switch to a contractionary policy, which would involve taking the opposite steps of expansionary policy, such as raising interest rates.

Even under ideal conditions, expansionary fiscal and monetary policy risk creating microeconomic distortions through the economy. Simple economic models often portray the effects of expansionary policy as neutral to the structure of the economy as if the money injected into the economy were distributed uniformly and instantaneously across the economy.

In actual practice, monetary and fiscal policy both operate by distributing new money to specific individuals, businesses, and industries who then spend and circulate the new money to the rest of the economy. Rather than uniformly boosting aggregate demand, this means that expansionary policy always involves an effective transfer of purchasing power and wealth from the earlier recipients to the later recipients of the new money.

In addition, like any government policy, an expansionary policy is potentially vulnerable to information and incentive problems. The distribution of the money injected by expansionary policy into the economy can obviously involve political considerations. Problems such as rent-seeking and principal-agent problems easily crop up whenever large sums of public money are up for grabs. And by definition, expansionary policy, whether fiscal or monetary, involves the distribution of large sums of public money.

Examples of Expansionary Policy

A major example of expansionary policy is the response following the 2008 financial crisis when central banks around the world lowered interest rates to near-zero and conducted major stimulus spending programs. In the United States, this included the American Recovery and Reinvestment Act and multiple rounds of quantitative easing by the U.S. Federal Reserve. U.S. policymakers spent and lent trillions of dollars into the U.S. economy in order to support domestic aggregate demand and prop up the financial system.

In a more recent example, declining oil prices from 2014 through the second quarter of 2016 caused many economies to slow down. Canada was hit especially hard in the first half of 2016, with almost one-third of its entire economy based in the energy sector. This caused bank profits to decline, making Canadian banks vulnerable to failure.

To combat these low oil prices, Canada enacted an expansionary monetary policy by reducing interest rates within the country. The expansionary policy was targeted to boost economic growth domestically.

However, the policy also meant a decrease in net interest margins for Canadian banks, squeezing bank profits.

Taylor Rule

What Is the Taylor Rule?

The Taylor rule (sometimes referred to as Taylor's rule or Taylor principle) is an econometric model that describes the relationship between Federal Reserve operating targets and the rates of inflation and gross domestic product growth. The Taylor rule has been interpreted both as a way to forecast Fed monetary policy and as a fixed rule policy to guide monetary policy in response to changes in economic conditions. The rule consists of a formula that relates the Fed's operating target for short-term interest rates to two factors: the deviation between actual and desired inflation rates and the deviation between real GDP growth and the desired GDP growth rates.

Understanding the Taylor Rule

In economics, Taylor's rule is essentially a forecasting model used to determine what interest rates should be to shift the economy toward stable prices and full employment. Taylor's rule makes the recommendation that the Federal Reserve should raise interest rates when inflation is high or when employment exceeds full employment levels. Conversely, when inflation and employment levels are low, the Taylor rule implies that interest rates should be decreased.

The Taylor rule was invented and published from 1992 to 1993 by John Taylor, a Stanford economist, who outlined the rule in his precedent-setting 1993 study "Discretion vs. Policy Rules in Practice."[1] Taylor continued to perfect the rule and made amendments to the formula in 1999.

The Taylor Rule Formula

Taylor's equation looks like: $r = p + 0.5y + 0.5(p - 2) + 2$
Where:
r = nominal fed funds rate
p = the rate of inflation
y = the percent deviation between current real GDP and the long-term linear trend in GDP

In simpler terms, this equation says that the Fed will adjust its fed funds rate target by an equally weighted average of the gap between actual inflation and the Fed's desired rate of inflation (assumed to be 2%) and the gap between observed real GDP and a hypothetical target GDP at a constant linear growth rate (calculated by Taylor at 2.2% from approximately 1984 to 1992). This means that the Fed will raise its target fed funds rate when inflation rises above 2% or real GDP growth rises above 2.2%, and lower the target rate when either of these falls below their respective targets.

The equation's purpose is to look at potential targets for interest rates; however, such a task is impossible without looking at inflation. To compare inflation and non-inflation rates, the total spectrum of an economy must be observed in terms of prices. Variations are often made to this formula based on what central bankers determine are the most important factors to include.

Other Considerations

For many, the jury is out on the Taylor rule as it comes with several drawbacks, the most serious being it cannot account for sudden shocks or turns in the economy, such as a stock or housing market crash. In his research and the original formulation of the rule, Taylor acknowledged this and pointed out that rigid adherence to a policy rule would not always be appropriate in the face of such shocks. Another shortcoming of the Taylor rule is that it can offer ambiguous advice if inflation and GDP growth move in opposite directions.

During periods of stagnant economic growth and high inflation, such as stagflation, the Taylor rule provides little guidance to policymakers, since the terms of the equation then tend to cancel each other out. While several issues with the rule are, as yet, unresolved, many central banks find the Taylor rule a favorable practice, and some research indicates that the use of similar rules may improve economic performance.

CHAPTER 5

Quantitative Easing Explained

The recent financial crisis and its aftermath have proven to be a great challenge for the Federal Reserve. In late 2008, in response to rapidly deteriorating economic and financial conditions, the Federal Open Market Committee (FOMC) pushed the federal funds rate target1 close to zero. As conditions worsened, the Fed turned to nontraditional policies to bolster financial market conditions. Such policies include large-scale asset purchases—in the hundreds of billions of dollars range—of, for example, mortgage-backed securities2 and Treasury securities. This action is commonly called "quantitative easing" (QE). Some believe QE will sharply increase inflation rates; however, these fears are not consistent with economic theory and empirical evidence—assuming the Fed is both willing and able to reverse QE as the recovery gains momentum.

Typically, the FOMC changes the federal funds rate target to achieve its dual mandate of maximum sus¬tainable economic growth and price stability. From September 2007 to June 2008, the FOMC incrementally lowered the federal funds rate target from 5.25 percent to 2 percent as turmoil engulfed credit markets. The financial panic intensified in mid- September 2008 when the investment banking company Lehman Brothers declared bankruptcy (the largest such filing in U.S. history) and American International Group (AIG) neared bankruptcy as its stock plummeted. In response, the Fed rolled out new emergency lending programs and lowered the federal funds rate target in October 2008 from 2 percent to 1 percent. In December 2008, the continuing severity of the crisis prompted the Fed to drop the target to the extraordinarily low range of between 0 and 0.25 percent, where it has remained. Because nominal interest rates cannot go below zero and the Fed needed to continue to support a weakened economy, it turned to nontraditional policy, including QE.

QE affects the economy through changes in interest rates on long-term Treasury securities and other financial instruments (e.g., corporate bonds). To have an appreciable impact on interest rates, QE requires large-scale asset purchases. When the Fed makes such purchases of, for example, Treasury securities, the result is an increased demand for those securities, which in turn raises their prices. Treasury prices and yields (interest rates) are inversely related: As prices increase, interest rates fall. As interest rates fall, the cost to businesses for financing capital investments, such as new equipment, decreases. Over time, new business investments should bolster economic activity, create new jobs, and reduce the unemployment rate. QE is not a new approach; it was used by the Fed in the 1930s,5 the Bank of Japan in 2001,6 and more recently by the Bank of England. Since 2009, the Fed has initiated QE two times, each with different goals.

The first round of QE began in March 2009 and concluded in March 2010. One of the primary goals was to increase the availability of credit in private markets to help revitalize mortgage lending and support the housing market. To accomplish this goal, the Fed purchased $1.25 trillion in mortgage-backed securities and $200 billion in federal agency debt (i.e., debt issued by Fannie Mae, Freddie Mac, and Ginnie Mae to fund the purchase of mortgage loans). To help lower interest rates in general (and thaw the frozen private credit market), the Fed also purchased $300 billion in long-term Treasury securities.

The second round of QE, widely called QE2, began in November 2010 and is scheduled to conclude by the end of the second quarter of 2011. Its goal is to strengthen the economic recovery and combat a possible Japanese-style deflationary outcome. QE2 works toward both of these objectives by fostering economic growth through lower interest rates intended to spur consumer spending and business investment. During QE2, the Fed will purchase up to $600 billion in long-term Treasury securities.

Critics of QE warn that because QE increases the monetary base8 significantly, dramatic inflation could result. Currently, banks hold a large number of reserves, which constitutes the largest component of the monetary base. If banks were to loan these reserves, they would effectively increase the money supply. If the money supply were to grow at a rapid rate, the resulting increase in economic activity could cause inflation to accelerate and expectations of future inflation to increase. The Fed, however, remains confident that its programs, including incentives for banks to retain their reserves, will prevent such an outcome.9 For example, the Fed pays banks interest on reserves at Fed banks. If the interest rate on these reserves is higher than the return banks could receive from alternative investments (the banks' opportunity cost), reserves will remain idle.

Public expectations of future inflation are also crucial in determining the path of inflation and the ultimate effect of QE. If the public trusts that the increase in the monetary base QE creates are only temporary, then they will not expect rapid inflation shortly. These expectations collectively influence actual pricing behavior and, in turn, actual inflation. As such, the credibility of the Federal Reserve is perhaps the most important determinant of successful monetary policy.

What did QE do?

Despite the title of the book, Friedman and Schwartz didn't document 100 years of the past for the sake of historical interest alone. They wanted to understand the effects of monetary policy.

Getting at these is harder than you might think because empirical economists can't do experiments. In a laboratory, a scientist interested in the effects of one thing on another - call them X and Y - can usually do two important things. He or she can "control" for - in other words, hold constant - everything else that might also affect Y. This allows one to isolate the study purely to what X does. It's also possible to move the "independent variable" X around at will, observing directly what it does to the "dependent variable" Y.

Empirical economists can't do either of these things. Policy changes are one of only many influences on the economy and it's not as if we can just switch these other things off. The best we can do is use large samples of data, coupled with various statistical methods, to even them out. And even if we could somehow freeze the rest of the world it would never be possible (or morally justifiable) than to experiment on it by arbitrarily putting up interest rates. The economy isn't a lab rat. What instead tends to happen, in the real world, is that policy reacts to events at least as much as it causes them. And it's this relationship from the economy to policy, rather than the other way around - that dominates the data. Friedman and Schwartz's study - the "narrative" method - was an effort to identify the rare occasions when this was not the case. They were trying to uncover natural experiments.

If these challenges exist for a conventional monetary policy they surely apply at least as much to QE. Our experience is more limited, the data sample therefore smaller. And the policy was very clearly a response to other events, in this case, the powerful contractionary forces unleashed by the banking crisis. This has hardly been a randomized trial.

So you cannot conclude from the fact of the recession of 2008-09, or the weak growth that followed, that QE was of no help. Alarmingly, things might have been that much worse without it. They certainly were in the Great Depression. Within three years of the Wall Street crash, the yield on US corporate bonds had risen to over 11%, even as the economy was collapsing; thousands of US banks failed, taking a third of deposits with them; industrial production halved and unemployment rose by over 20% points.

Equally, there were many other differences between the last financial crisis and the Great Depression, so we can't on the face of it give QE all the credit for having avoided that fate. There was no deposit insurance during the early 1930s, something that surely contributed to the widespread runs on banks and their subsequent failure. In 2008-09, as well as conducting QE, central banks cut interest rates close to zero and engaged in direct collateralized lending to the banking system. Governments also provided support to the banking system, via equity bailouts and lending schemes of their own. They also eased fiscal policy more aggressively and managed to avoid the protectionist measures that had exacerbated the Great Depression. To a greater or lesser extent, all these things must have helped.

So, what can we say about the specific contribution of QE? We may not be able to employ their "narrative" method, nor is our experience of QE as extensive as for more conventional monetary policy. But we do have some advantages over Friedman and Schwartz. We have more data than they did, including a lot of high-frequency information on the behavior of financial markets. This allows us to see the reaction of asset prices to QE announcements over short periods, cutting down on extraneous influences. We also have more advanced statistical techniques, helping to refine the estimates of the effects on economic activity.

I won't go into all this work in any great detail. (For that you can read a very good and comprehensive survey by Andy Haldane and other Bank economists and the references therein.) Let me just try and summarise what it says:

First, and all else equal, asset purchases do seem to have had a significant impact on economic activity. Some studies get at that effect using existing estimates of the sensitivity of GDP to bond yields and combining those with the impact of QE announcements on those yields. Others estimate the impact on bond markets and activity jointly.

There is some suggestion in Haldane et al (2016) that the early phases of asset purchases had more powerful effects, and it's clear that the biggest daily moves in bond yields occurred after the very first QE announcements in early 2009. But on average, and whichever method one uses, there does seem to have been a significant effect on demand. The central estimate in Weale and Wieladek (2016), for example, is that purchases worth 1% of GDP boost UK GDP by around 0.25%.

Second, if the effect on long-term bond yields is clear, the impact on share prices is harder to detect. On some days after QE announcements equity prices went up - the largest rise happened to be after the extension of asset purchases in October 2011, when gilt yields actually went up - but on others, they fell. That doesn't prove there was no impact. By their nature, the prices of risky assets are more volatile. Such was the flow of negative news about the economy and corporate profits in 2009, even from day to day, that equity markets often weakened even as bond markets strengthened.

But it should be borne in mind when reading - as one often does - that QE has done little except boosted prices of assets like shares and houses, or even led to a "boom" or "bubble" in those markets. The average annual growth of UK house prices over rolling 10-year periods. The latest figure is 2%. That's less than household income growth over the past decade. It's also close to the lowest rate of growth over any ten years since the period following the Second World War. The peak rate of 18% a year was during the 1970s.

QE1 had the largest impact on yields

Gilt reaction (basis points)

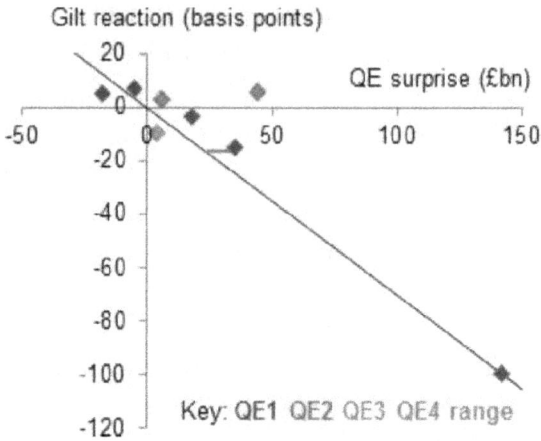

Key: QE1 QE2 QE3 QE4 range

The impact on share prices is harder to detect

Reaction, per cent

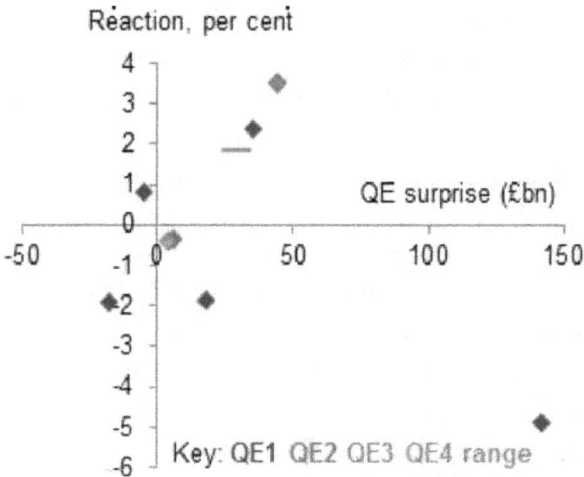

Key: QE1 QE2 QE3 QE4 range

House prices haven't risen much over the past 10 years

Per cent

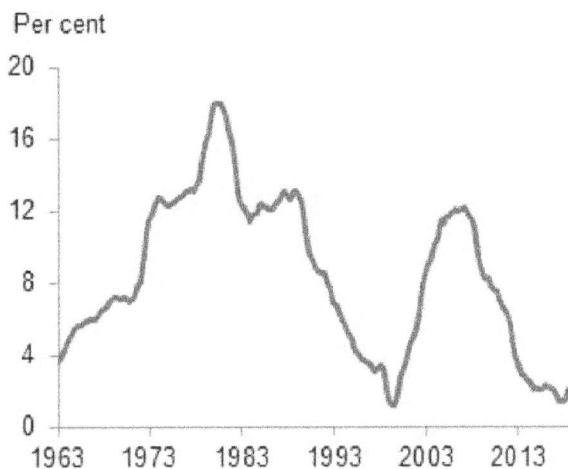

Real equity prices well below pre-crisis levels

Indices, 2005Q1=100

Real house prices
Real UK-facing equity prices

Real equity prices and de-trended GDP

Index, 2005Q1=100 — Per cent deviation from trend

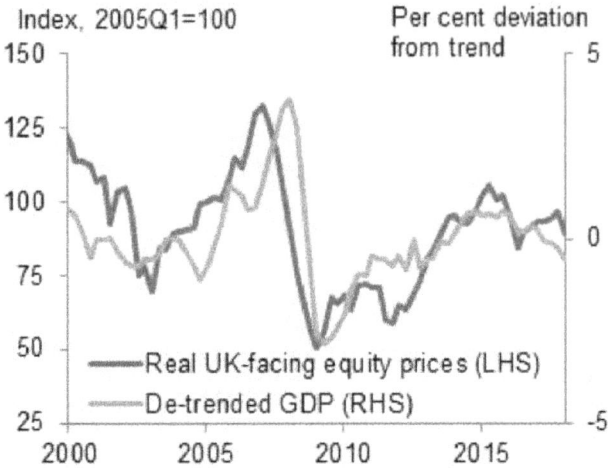

Real UK-facing equity prices (LHS)
De-trended GDP (RHS)

The general level of inflation was also very high at that time: every price was going up rapidly. It's, therefore, more informative to look at asset prices in real terms (i.e. relative to consumer prices). The level of real house prices is plotted in blue in Chart 5. As you can see, they went up extremely rapidly between 1996 and 2004. But the latest figure is barely any higher than it was in the middle of the last decade. As for shares, real equity prices of UK-facing companies (in red) are still 30% lower than immediately before the financial crisis (and almost as far below the earlier peak in the late 1990s).

As I say, we can't conclude from all this that QE had no impact at all on these prices, even at the margin. Given its effects on longer-term interest rates, and on economic activity, it probably did. But their apparent lack of response does at least demonstrate that the policy had quite a bit to fight against. To the extent there was such an effect, it would be more accurate to say QE helped to prevent these prices from falling further, rather than that it fuelled any sort of "boom".

You can tell the same story about QE and the wider economy. All else equal, the policy supported demand, activity, and employment. But that support was being provided in the face of significant contractionary forces, arising from both the first phase of the financial crisis and then its unwelcome offspring, the euro area crisis of 2010-12. You can see from Chart 6 that it wasn't until confidence in the single currency was restored in mid-20128, and a more sustained economic recovery began in the UK (the green line is de-trended GDP9), that these assets prices also recovered.

Why The Impact Of QE Might Be Changeable

Estimates of how QE has affected the economy often assume the effect is invariant: so many pounds of QE means such-and-such an impact on GDP, no matter what else is going on. Yet our experience so far suggests the effect may not be fixed. In particular, it seems to have been larger when QE was first launched than in subsequent rounds. If that can only be a tentative conclusion from the UK experience what's happened more recently in the US is surely more striking.

As you know, the Fed has now started to reduce its asset holdings: it has embarked on what you might call "QT" (T for tightening).

Given the sizeable impact of QE1, including in the US, you might have expected this to result in a material rise in bond yields, especially at a time when the US government is also starting to sell more debt. The first column in Chart 7 gives you some idea of the predicted effect on this basis. It takes the median projection for the decline in the size of its balance sheet over the next three years (as calculated by the New York Fed). It then multiplies that by the estimated response of Treasury yields, per dollar of purchases, in the first phase of QE.11

US QT has done little to US bond yields

Basis points

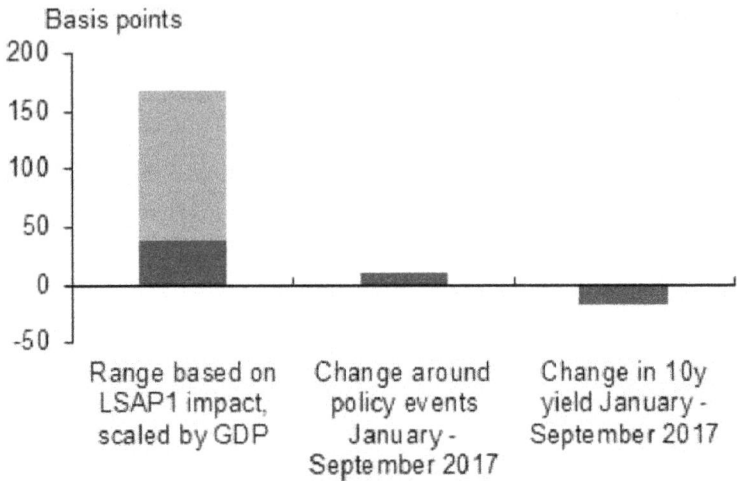

Range based on LSAP1 impact, scaled by GDP	Change around policy events January - September 2017	Change in 10y yield January - September 2017

In the event, things have turned out rather differently. Despite the various QT announcements in the first nine months of last year (and despite rising short rates and easier fiscal policy) yields fell over that period (the right-hand bar). That, of course, might be due to any number of other influences. But even if you focus on the particular points at which the policy was communicated12 (the middle bar) there was essentially no reaction in the government bond market.

Why Might This Be?

One thing that might have amplified QE's impact when it was first used was its sheer novelty value. Once markets discover the policy is feasible, perhaps the premium required for holding longer-term bonds is permanently lowered, if only to a small extent.

But there are potentially more important reasons why the later rounds of QE - and in particular the early stages of QT - have had smaller effects. These are connected with the various ways in which QE actually works. To understand why it's worth stepping back and reminding ourselves what the mechanics of the policy actually are.

QE is sometimes described as "printing money". That can be a helpful piece of shorthand. It can also be a misleading one. It risks giving the impression that the central bank simply hands out wads of cash, getting nothing in return. I've often heard, in particular, that QE involves "giving" money to the banks.

What actually happens is this (there's a stylized depiction at the back of this speech): the central bank buys government bonds, mainly from non-banks, on the open market. Imagine we pay for them with a cheque. The seller of the gilt lodges the cheque at its own commercial bank, increasing the size of its deposit holdings; that commercial bank, in its turn, sends the cheque back to us, increasing its deposits at the central bank (so-called "reserves"). And there's no direct effect on anyone's net financial position. The seller of the gilt ends up with more money in its bank account but no change in its total assets. The two banks, of the commercial and central variety, end up with larger balance sheets but the rises in assets and liabilities are of equal size.

So perhaps a more accurate description of the process is that it replaces one liability of the consolidated public sector (longer-term government bonds) with another (deposits at the central bank). The effect is to depress the average maturity of those consolidated liabilities. And you might wonder, especially since both bonds and reserves pay interest, why this should do anything at all. Indeed, there's a famous neutrality result in finance, originally applied to corporate balance sheets, that says exactly this. Under certain conditions, when financial markets are functioning smoothly, pure financial transactions of this sort do nothing. At least in this idealized theoretical setting, it makes no difference to its overall cost of capital if a firm issues interest-bearing debt and buy back its own shares. The maturity profile of government debt wouldn't matter for bond yields. And, viewing central bank money simply as the shortest-maturity liability that the public sector can issue, nor would those yields respond to open-market operations by the central bank (QE).15 This is what Ben Bernanke was getting at when he quipped that QE is something that "works in practice but doesn't work in theory".

So why does it work in practice - why has it had noticeable effects on bond yields (albeit to varying degrees)? I'm not to go into any great detail here. There are masses of stuff you can read - if you wish to - about the various mechanisms involved.16 Economists have generally focussed on three. The "bank lending" channel emphasizes the importance of banks' liquid assets and the potential constraints that a lack of reserves can impose on their behavior, including their appetite to lend. The "portfolio balance" channel, generally reckoned to be more important after the 2008-09 financial crisis, stresses the direct price effects on the assets purchased by the central bank, and sets out what's necessary for these to exist. (What's usually required, in one form or another, is that holders of long-dated assets have "preferred habitats", and can be persuaded to move out of them - to sell those assets - only by a rise in prices.) The third - the potential "signaling" effect - says what matters is what QE says about the central bank's intentions regarding future policy and in particular the likely path of official interest rates.

The point I want to make here is that all three can change. One might even say this is intrinsic to the effects involved.

The first two - the "bank lending" and "portfolio balance" channels - rely, in their different ways, on markets being sufficiently imperfect that the neutrality result no longer applies. But markets are more impaired at some times than others. Before the crisis, many financial assets were considered liquid. They could be easily traded, prices were readily quoted and investors would happily switch between them, even in response to relatively small changes in their relative price. The demand for central bank money was lower - why would you need it if liquidity was easily available elsewhere? - and "preferred habitats" weaker.

In that environment, shifts in the central bank's balance sheet may not have had much effect. It was when things started to seize up, and markets became more dysfunctional, that these transactions mattered. With fewer assets considered liquid, the demand for central bank money went up. With preferred habitats more entrenched, the effect of asset purchases on prices was larger. You might therefore have expected QE, at least through these channels, to have become more important. Conversely, you might also expect their impact to diminish once more normal market conditions are restored. While he was on the MPC my former colleague David Miles gave a very clear and more detailed explanation of this point (Miles (2014)).

As for the third, it surely makes sense that the strength of the "signalling effect" - what markets infer from QE decisions about future interest rates, and the central bank's intentions regarding its overall policy stance - depends on what it communicates alongside its decision.

In the early phases of QE, the policy was seen as an aggressive attempt to ease monetary conditions for an extended period. Whatever else it might have done to depress the "term premium" - the extra yield required by long-maturity bondholders, even above their expectations of future short-term interest rates - it also lowered those rate expectations. QE and forward interest rates were effectively used in a complementary fashion, pushing in the same direction.

Something similar occurred, albeit in the opposite direction, when the Fed suggested in 2013 that it might reduce the pace of its asset purchases (the so-called "taper tantrum"). This wasn't yet QT - nor, in the Congressional testimony that triggered the reaction, did Fed Chair Ben Bernanke refers directly to future interest rates ("If we see continued improvement [in the economy] and we have confidence that that is going to be sustained then we could, in the next few meetings, take a step down in our pace of [asset] purchases").19 But it was taken as a sign of a more hawkish stance overall: because the Fed was getting more optimistic about the economy, QE would be tapered and, the markets judged, official interest rates would also begin to rise earlier than previously expected. As a result, and although the move was reversed within a few months, US bond yields also rose significantly.

The communication around the Fed's "QT" policy was rather different. When in the early part of last year it first signalled its intention to start shrinking the balance sheet later in 2017, the FOMC went out of its way to say that, to the extent, the policy tightened monetary conditions, official interest rates would be that much lower than they otherwise would have been. This is how Janet Yellen put it in a speech in January 2017: "The downward pressure on longer-term interest rates that the Fed's asset holdings exert is expected to diminish over time -- a development that amounts to a "passive" removal of monetary policy accommodation. Other things being equal, this argues for a more gradual approach to raising short-term rates".

In other words, rate rises and any tightening effect of shrinking the balance sheet should be seen as substitutes. More of the latter would mean less of the former, and the overall stance of policy - the balance sheet and official interest rates taken together - would be whatever it needed to be to meet the Fed's remit, given the economic conditions prevailing at the time. Compared with the "taper tantrum" episode this sent a different message about the overall stance of policy and I suspect that played a part in dampening the impact of QT announcements on longer-term bond yields.

The MPC's Approach To Unwinding QE

In time the QE will also start to be unwound in the UK. The MPC set out its basic framework for this process some time ago, in the November 2015 Inflation Report. We said then that we would begin to start reducing the stock of QE only once the official Bank Rate had risen some way. This was partly because the conventional policy is more flexible, better suited to responding to shorter-term economic fluctuations. It was also a response to the relatively higher degree of uncertainty about the effect of changes in the stock of QE.

I've discussed this at some length today. The smaller sample means estimates of the impact of unconventional policy are bound to be less precise. If that's the case when the impact is unchangeable it can only be truer still if it varies according to economic conditions. But even in 2015, the MPC felt sufficiently confident in its assessment of what changes in interest rates do - more so, in particular, than in the estimated impact of changes in QE - that it said would prefer to use Bank Rate as the "marginal" or "primary" instrument of policy. That means getting Bank Rate to a level from which it could be cut ("materially") as well as raised. The US Fed subsequently adopted a similar approach, saying that rises in official interest rates should be "well underway" before the unwind process began.

At the time of that initial guidance our version of "well underway" was judged to mean a Bank Rate of "around 2%". Since then we have also reduced our estimate of the effective lower bound for interest rates (thanks in part to the effectiveness of the Term Funding Scheme, part of the package of measures put in place in August 2016, we now think we can safely cut Bank Rate close to zero, if necessary). So when we updated the guidance this summer, in the June Monetary Policy Summary, we lowered the estimated threshold to "around 1.5%". We don't know exactly when that will be. But the framework is designed to ensure that, should inflationary pressures weaken after that date, the first response would be to cut interest rates.

In principle, those disinflationary influences might include the process of QE unwinding itself. To that extent, Bank Rate would be lower than it otherwise would have been. That's why we took care to add another sentence to last month's MPS: "Decisions on Bank Rate will take into account any impact of changes in the stock of purchased assets on overall monetary conditions, in order to achieve the inflation target".

In some ways this is no more than the phrase "primary instrument of policy" implies. As long as they're free to do so, interest rates will always move around to offset things that affect inflation - in both directions, and wherever those influences come from. But we were also aware of the US experience and the Fed's careful communication around QT.

QE has often been described as a "new-fangled" policy, something that involves "printing money" and has served only to engineer large rises in the prices of financial and other assets, benefiting only the better off.

Broadly speaking I don't think any of these things are true. It's not new; it's not exactly printing money; equity and house prices are in real terms still comfortably below their pre-crisis levels; inequality hasn't risen - nor, according to the most detailed analysis available, did easier monetary policy have any net impact on it.

To be sure, asset prices would probably have fallen further had QE and other measures not been put in place in 2009. The same goes for the economy itself. As far as we can tell, asset purchases provided significant support to aggregate demand, even if it wasn't enough to offset fully the extended contractionary effects of the crisis. Perhaps Friedman and Schwartz over-emphasised the failures of the US Fed as a cause of the Great Depression. But I don't think anyone can reasonably argue it was worth risking those same mistakes a second time.

Later rounds of QE may have been less effective than the first. In the US, where the Fed has begun to shrink its balance sheet, its "QT" announcements appear to have had very little impact. At least in part, that's likely to be by design. The pace of unwinding is very gradual. And the FOMC emphasized that to the extent a shrinking balance sheet tightened monetary conditions the official interest rate would be commensurately lower (than it would otherwise have been). The overall stance of policy would be set to ensure the central bank meets its objectives.

The same is true here. Our task remains to hit the inflation target and we will always seek to ensure that the combined effects of the APF and more conventional changes in Bank Rate are set to that end.

The Significance of QE

As the above definition states, quantitative easing is simply the addition of additional money supply into the system. This is significant because it is only in recent years that all the prosperous central bankers across the world have started doing this. Banks like the Federal Reserve, the European Central Bank, and the Bank of Japan all used interest rates to regulate the economy. For instance, in case of credit was tight and banks were not lending enough, these central banks would simply cut the rates to boost lending. They would do the exact opposite and raise rates when there was excess lending going on and there was danger of inflation.

However, in the crisis of 2008, these measures did not seem to be working. All the aforementioned Central Banks had almost slashed their interest rates to zero! Yet they were not able to spur lending. It is then that the banks turned to quantitative easing.

The Methodology

When central banks use quantitative easing, they inject money into and remove money from the economy as required. For instance, they can have a target amount of lending that needs to be done and a target inflation rate that needs to be met. In case, the inflation is too low but so is the lending, the central banks can create new money using quantitative easing and then buy new assets. The basic premise is that the Fed does not buy bonds from already existing money rather the Fed creates new money when it makes these purchases. The new money supply drops the lending rate of the existing money and is theoretically supposed to boost the lending in the economy and therefore cause an increase in the economic activity.

Asset Purchase Program

Quantitative easing involves central banks buying large quantities of assets from the market. The central bank buys these assets with the money that it creates. Therefore the amount of assets that the Fed buys is the amount of money that has been pumped into the system.

For instance, consider the case of the massive bailout of 2008. Before 2008, the Feds balance sheet stood at $880 billion. This meant that the amount of money that the Fed pumped into the system for all these years stood at $880 billion. Then, it started quantitative easing and by the year 2015, the Feds balance sheet stood at over $4 trillion. The Fed had almost raised the money supply by five times in that very short time frame.

Fractional Reserve Banking

All the money that is created by the Fed for these asset purchases is high-powered money. This means that this money is used as reserves by the banks based on which they can expand the money supply even more. Thus, for every dollar that is issued by the Federal Reserve to buy bonds in the name of quantitative easing, several more dollars end up in circulation in the market through the use of fractional reserve banking. Hence, the Federal Reserve is capable of causing severe inflation through its asset purchase program. In fact, there is a prevailing viewpoint amongst critics that the Fed has used these expansionary policies to artificially prop up all the asset markets and hide its failure from the subprime mortgage crisis.

Quantum of the Issue

The sheer scale of quantitative easing makes it a mind-boggling affair. Now, we already know that the Federal Reserve's balance sheet has grown by a factor of 5 in the 7 years post the subprime crisis! This is because the Fed is pumping $85 billion into the market each month through asset purchases. The Fed buys US Treasury bonds from whichever bank can offer it to them at the lowest rate.

The problem is that now the US government, the Treasury, and the Federal Reserve want to put an end to quantitative easing. However, the market has literally grown dependant on the liquidity shots that are provided by quantitative easing. Hence, if the Fed were to stop buying bonds now, it would end up creating a severe demand shortage in the markets since its $85 billion per month purchases create significant demand in the market.

Therefore, the issue of quantitative easing is today at the heart of international financial matters and is highly discussed by global bodies such as World Bank and IMF! Markets all across the world are connected to the United States. Hence any policy change in the US pertaining to this policy of quantitative easing is likely to have global ramifications. Therefore, the world has its eyes set on how this policy is finally going to play out!

Quantitative Easing Tapering - Meaning & Its Importance

What Does Quantitative Easing (QE) Tapering Mean?

Quantitative easing (QE) means increasing the money supply of the system. This is done when the Central Bank creates new money and uses the money to make asset purchases. These asset purchases inject the new money into the system.

Quantitative easing (QE) tapering is the reverse policy of quantitative easing (QE). It is when the government stops following the policy of quantitative easing (QE) gradually. For instance, at the present moment, the US government is buying $85 billion worth of assets monthly. If the US government were to drop the asset purchases from $85 billion to $60 billion the next month, that would amount to quantitative easing (QE) tapering.

The Fed has been contemplating quantitative easing (QE) tapering for all of 2014. However, even the slightest mention of quantitative easing (QE) tapering sends the markets crashing. It is for this reason that the Fed is holding on and trying to find a better way and time to deal with the situation.

Why is Quantitative Easing (QE) Tapering Important?

The policy of quantitative easing (QE) tapering has been talked about almost every day in the American media and the rest of the world. This is because it is the most important and the most unheard-of monetary policy of our times. The magnitude of this policy is what provides it with this much importance. The way this policy's implications unravel will have a long-lasting and profound impact on various economic parameters. A summary of this has been provided in this article.

Interest Rates: The first and foremost impact of quantitative easing (QE) tapering will be seen on interest rates. The impact is almost immediate. In fact, quantitative easing (QE) is generally used when the interest rates are already at zero level and yet the Central Bank wants to provide even more stimulus. Hence quantitative easing (QE) can be thought of as a sub-zero interest rate policy. The quantitative easing (QE) policy, therefore, lowers the interest rate when introduces. At the present moment, it has been present in the market for the past 5 years and the market has grown used to it. Hence, when the policy of quantitative easing (QE) tapering is adopted, it is expected to send the interest rates shooting. This is because a limited money supply means lenders will have to ration their lending. They will lend out money to those who can offer the highest interest rates and this competition will send the interest rates skyrocketing.

Inflation and Deflation: The policy of quantitative easing (QE) is inflationary. This is because it simply increases the monetary base in the economy. Therefore, when there is more money available and it is chasing relatively fewer goods, inflation occurs and prices skyrocket. The United States has undergone three rounds of massive quantitative easing (QE) and the prices there are grossly inflated compared to what they would have been without the quantitative easing (QE) policy.

Hence, when the opposite policy of quantitative easing (QE) tapering is implemented, inflation is likely to turn into deflation. This is because quantitative easing (QE) tapering pulls money out of the system. Hence there is now less money (as compared to before) chasing the goods available, making every good less expensive.

Employment: As we already know that employment is closely linked to that state of inflation or deflation in the economy. When there is excess money in the economy, the confidence is upbeat, more and more goods are being produced. Therefore, as a result, more and more people get employed in the economy. Therefore quantitative easing (QE) is positively correlated to a higher employment level.

On the contrary, when there is less money in the economy, consumer confidence is low, people are making fewer purchases, and hence producers are producing fewer goods. Thus, a lower money supply results in a downfall in employment levels. Therefore, a policy of quantitative easing (QE) tapering results in lower employment.

GDP: The amount of goods produced within an economy adds up to be its Gross Domestic Product (GDP). There is therefore a clear correlation between the amount of money supply in the system and the Gross Domestic Product (GDP). When quantitative easing (QE) is set into motion, the GDP of an economy goes up and the economy reaches the boom phase in the economic cycle. On the contrary, when the policy of quantitative easing (QE) tapering is set into motion, the GDP of an economy goes down and pushes the economy into a recession.

Asset Prices: The money supply of any economy is linked to its asset prices. As the money supply increases, everybody in the economy has more purchasing power and asset prices tend to go up.

However, when the money supply decreases, the reverse happens and asset prices tend to deflate. In the case of quantitative easing (QE) tapering, this is exactly what is expected to happen. The Fed has artificially inflated the dollar money supply by creating money and buying assets from the market. Currently, this is an ongoing policy and when the Fed decides to stop doing this, the money supply will fall causing the asset markets to contract. This will lead to an immense transfer of wealth in the population as everybody is invested in these markets to different degrees.

Quantitative easing (QE) tapering, therefore, is expected to have a huge impact on all the markets in the world. Since there is not much historical precedent, people are waiting to see the result of the use of this policy.

Advantages of Quantitative Easing

The strategy of quantitative easing is a new tool being used by Central Banks all over the world. Most big central banks like the Fed, Central Bank of England, European Central Bank, and the Bank of Japan have been using this strategy extensively as of late. This tool has been used on such a grand scale that there is a belief that if the consequences do not work out as intended, it could bring down the entire system along with it. So then what is it that is keeping the governments and the central banks hooked to the use of quantitative easing? In this article, we will have a look at some of the advantages of quantitative easing:

Additional Tool

Quantitative easing is a new tool that is at the disposal of the Central Bankers. Earlier, the Central Bankers could only resort to interest rate changes to influence the economy. For instance, when the economy was low, they would lower the interest rates, spurring lending and other economic activity. They would do the converse when the economy was high and needed to be brought down.

However, in recent crises like the ones in Japan and the United States, the interest rates had already been reduced to sub-zero levels. Hence, the government had no probable course of action, in case they wanted to spur the economy. In cases like these, quantitative easing (QE) comes in handy. This is because it acts as an additional tool in the kit of the government and helps the Central Bankers mitigate crises when they happen.

Lowers Interest Rates

The main effect of quantitative easing (QE) is that it increases the monetary base i.e. the money supply of the system. A higher money supply has always been linked to a fall in interest rates. This is because excess money starts flowing into the system and then lenders have to compete with each other to lend that excess money. In the process of this competition, they drag the interest rates down. Hence, quantitative easing (QE) as a tool becomes double as effective. By introducing quantitative easing (QE) the other objective of monetary policy i.e. to lower interest rates is automatically achieved! A lower interest rate further supports an expansionary monetary policy causing the boom phase to grow bigger. In the short run, quantitative easing (QE) may almost seem like it is too good to be true.

Prevents Unemployment

Economic crises are usually followed by epic unemployment. For instance, the Great Depression of 1929 is one of the worst periods in economic history. More than 40% of the people were unemployed during that time. The unemployment stretched for many years before the economy became normal. However, in modern-day crises, unemployment has seldom been seen stretching so long and affecting so many people. This can be partly attributed to the economic policy of quantitative easing (QE). This policy has ensured that the employment rates do not fall so drastically so stay down for so long. Hence, in the short run, the policy of quantitative easing (QE) has been extremely beneficial to the average person because it has protected their jobs. Otherwise, the crisis of 2008 was enough to create a prolonged period of unemployment.

Drains Toxic Assets

In the policy of quantitative easing (QE), the Central Bank buys assets from the open market. It does so by using newly created money and hence injects this money into the system. Now, the assets purchased by the central bank could be anything. Usually, they are government bonds because this increases the liquidity of the market for government bonds and also because they tend to be the safest. However, in cases like the subprime mortgages, the government could have also purchased the toxic assets via a quantitative easing (QE) program. This drains the toxic assets out of the system and puts them in closed vaults of the central bank. Once the crisis begins to resolve itself, these toxic assets are slowly released into the economy wherein they can be quickly absorbed and do not disturb the equilibrium of the entire economy.

Immediate Results

The best part about the policy of quantitative easing (QE) is that it provides immediate results. As and when a crisis hits the economy, the government can simply start quantitative easing. As a result, quantitative easing is considered to be the most preferred solution by governments all over the world. This is because it can be easily applied as a quick fix. It might be a sad thing to know but the economic policies of the world are decided based on political motives. Therefore, quantitative easing which is a great political strategy since like the painkillers it provides instant relief from the problems is considered to be highly effective.

Government Control

Another plus point that works in favor of quantitative easing is the fact that the government has virtually 100% control over the outcomes. In case the central bank cuts interest rates, it is then dependent on the member banks to pass on these interest rate cuts to the final consumers in the form of increased lending. However, in the case of quantitative easing, the government has 100% control over the outcome of the exercise. Since they are buying bonds, they know the exact amount of money that they are circulating in the marketplace and how it will affect employment, consumer confidence, and the economy as a whole.

These perceived benefits are what make quantitative easing one of the most preferred methods of monetary interference by the Central Banks today. However, these benefits have been highly critiqued and questioned and many feel that there are no advantages to quantitative easing, rather there are massive disadvantages.

Disadvantages of Quantitative Easing

The goal of the monetary policy of any economy is to provide stability. That is the purpose for which the central banks were created in the first place. The charter of each of the central banks like the Fed, Bank of England, and Bank of Japan mention fiscal stability as their number one objective. However, critics believe that policies such as quantitative easing work in the opposite direction. In the short term, they provide monetary stimulus. However, in the long run, they create monetary instability which defeats the entire purpose of having a central bank. In this article, we will have a closer look at some more criticisms of the quantitative easing policy.

Inflation

The goal of the central banks is to keep inflation at a bare minimum. However, the policy of quantitative easing does the exact opposite. Since this policy creates money and uses this money to further amplify lending by using this money as reserves, it is inherently inflationary. There is not much empirical evidence about the quantum of inflation that is caused by quantitative easing. This is because quantitative easing is a relatively recent phenomenon. However, the economic policy suggests that quantitative easing will be used in a depressed economy and therefore the first effects of inflation will be good as they will stimulate the economy. The later effects of such stimulation will be difficult to manage when the economy recovers. Therefore, it is highly likely that quantitative easing solves one problem but creates another in the next few years. It is therefore only a temporary quick fix and not a long-term solution.

Interest Rates

Like inflation, the goal of the central banks is to keep the interest rates at somewhat stable levels. The more fluctuation there is in the interest rates in the economy, the worse is the performance of the central bank. It is stability that brings about strong consumer confidence which in turn brings about a strong economy. On the other hand, if prices fluctuate wildly, consumers do not feel the same level of confidence and the economy gets depressed in the long run as consumers tend to delay spending and avoid purchases.

The policy of quantitative easing brings about a fall in the interest rates in the short run. However, in the long run, it leads to inflation which causes the interest rates to rise causing the exact opposite of financial stability.

Therefore, critics of quantitative easing believe that it is a disruptive policy that creates negative effects on the economy.

Business Cycles

Many critics believe that quantitative easing is the culprit behind the creation of the business cycles. They believe that quantitative easing creates easy money in the economy. This money then reaches lenders who want to lend it out at any cost. They compete amongst themselves to find borrowers. In the process of this competition, they end up lending money to people who shouldn't have received the loans in the first place. Therefore, the policy of quantitative easing first creates a boom i.e. an expansionary phase wherein the banks are lending money to everyone and when all businesses are growing.

However, later the same monetary policy leads to deleveraging by the banks. This is because when quantitative easing stops, money becomes tight. This causes banks to call in their loans and as a result, businesses start contracting i.e. a recession ensues. Therefore the same policy of quantitative easing caused both the boom as well the recession phase in the economy!

Employment

Employment is closely linked with the business cycles. The boom phase witnesses the massive creation of employment. Banks lend easy money to businesses and they then use this money to expand, creating jobs in the process. Thus, the use of quantitative easing does create jobs in the short run. However, in the process, the economy gets used to growing only after receiving monetary injections from the central bank. Therefore, as and when the bond-buying stops so do the bank lending, and businesses start to contract. It is a well-known fact that as and when businesses contract, they reduce the number of employees that they can hire. As a result, people get fired and therefore employment levels plummet. Once again, quantitative easing was supposed to stabilize the employment rate. Instead, it destabilized it by first raising it and then making it fall.

Asset Bubbles

An abundance of money always creates bubbles in the asset markets. Higher salaries and higher profits always find their way into these markets raising the prices of assets that are traded in them. Therefore the policy of quantitative easing leads to an asset bubble forming in the market. Once again, the market, like the economy in general becomes hooked to the increasing amounts of monetary stimulus that are received on a day-to-day basis, and once this stimulus stops people start pulling their money out of the markets causing the prices to crash. Thus, the policy of quantitative easing could lead to an increase as well as a sudden crash in the market prices bringing about huge transfers of wealth.

The theory of quantitative easing is therefore relatively untested. There are big arguments on both sides of this theory. Some people believe that it is extremely useful whereas others believe that it is dangerous and can bring down entire economies.

Effect of Quantitative Easing on Stock Markets

Quantitative easing (QE) affects a lot of areas within the economy. However, one of the most important effects occurs in the stock markets. The recent rounds of quantitative easing (QE) by the Fed lead to a lot of volatility in the stock market. Prices rose and dropped in value on the news of quantitative easing (QE). However, investors who were not well versed with this policy because of its short history were left curious as to what is happening and why. This led many experts to come up with many theories as to why this is happening. This article will explain the various viewpoints that have arisen in the past few years regarding the relationship between quantitative easing (QE) and the stock markets.

Mainstream Point of View

The mainstream point of view suggests that the effect of quantitative easing (QE) is pretty straightforward in the stock markets. When there is an expansionary quantitative easing (QE) policy announced, the market becomes bullish and stock prices begin to go up. On the other hand, quantitative easing (QE) tapering contracts the economy, then the markets become bearish and stocks tend to go down in value.

The logic behind this is said to be relatively simple too. Well, according to mainstream economists, quantitative easing (QE) uplifts a depressed economy. Therefore, investors see it as a sign of better times ahead and make a beeline to buy the stocks expecting growth in the markets. However, the corollary of the same theory would also mean that investors will react negatively to a quantitative easing (QE) tapering program. The execution of a quantitative easing (QE) tapering is likely to cause a drastic fall in the value of stocks because it may mean that investors would have to look forward to times that are hard for business.

Therefore, the theory speaks for itself. In the short run, quantitative easing (QE) causes a boom. However, since quantitative easing (QE) cannot continue forever, sooner or later, quantitative easing (QE) ends causing a bust in the economy.

Debasement Point of View

Contradictory to the mainstream view of quantitative easing (QE) is the debasement point of view. The conclusions of the debasement point of view are also similar to that of the mainstream point of view. However, the rationale behind the conclusions varies widely.

The debasement point of view believes that quantitative easing (QE) is injecting money into the system. The new money derives its value because of the loss of purchasing power of the old money in circulation. Therefore, the markets adjust their prices to reflect this phenomenon. For instance, the stocks rise in value when the news of a quantitative easing (QE) occurs. This is because as quantitative easing (QE) occurs money loses its value and therefore more money is required to buy the same goods. On the other hand, when news of quantitative easing (QE) tapering occurs, the stocks fall in value when quantitative easing (QE) tapering occurs since this reduces the money supply and hence increases the real value of money. According to the debasement point of view, the rise and fall in the stock market are actually due to fluctuating value of money and has got nothing to do with the value of stocks.

Expansionary Point of View

The expansionary point of view regarding quantitative easing (QE) also states that quantitative easing (QE) makes the economy go upwards whereas the lack of quantitative easing (QE) makes it spiral downwards.

The logic behind this is based on the changes which happen in the real economy.

For instance, when there is more money in the system, people will buy more goods and services. This translates into higher demand which further translates into even higher demand. Therefore, because of the increasing demand companies tend to prosper and as a result, the stock market goes up.

The fall in stock values as a result of the quantitative easing (QE) tapering can be explained similarly. When money is sucked out of the system, the demand is depressed and employment is reduced which further affects confidence and leads to more depression in the economy. Therefore, companies witness falling sales and as a result, the stock market goes down in value.

Interest Rates Point of View

The last point of view that we will be discussing is based on interest rates. It is a combination of multiple other theories. This point of view believes that quantitative easing (QE) causes the real interest rates in the economy to drop. As a result, when quantitative easing (QE) is announced, demand goes up, employment goes up and so the stock markets go up. However, it identifies interest rates drop as being the critical factor in the boom phase. For instance, if somehow quantitative easing (QE) did not lead to a real interest rate drop, it would not cause a boom in the economy.

The same logic can be further extended to explain the downturn that follows when quantitative easing (QE) tapering takes place. According to this theory, markets become depressed only because the real interest rate rises. Everything else is merely a side effect of the rising interest rates.

Thus the theories are unanimous about the effect of quantitative easing (QE). There is no doubt about the fact that an expansionary quantitative easing (QE) causes the market to rise whereas a decision to undergo quantitative easing (QE) tapering makes it drop. The causes that lead to this effect are believed to be different by different theories.

Quantitative Easing and the Bond Market

Of all the markets in the world that are being affected by the policy of quantitative easing (QE) tapering, the bond markets are the most affected. This is because the policy rules mandate that the primary investments being made by the government as a result of the money created must be in the bond markets. As a result, a massive amount of money is entering and leaving the bond market based on the changes in this policy.

In this article, we will have a closer look at the effects of both quantitative easing (QE) as well as quantitative easing (QE) tapering on the bond market.

Effects of Quantitative Easing

Quantitative easing (QE) has many effects on the market. The foremost ones which have the highest impact have been listed in this article.

Increased Demand: The bond markets around the world and particularly the ones in the US and Europe face the most direct impact of the quantitative easing (QE) policies being launched by governments across the world. This is because quantitative easing (QE), by definition, refers to the buying of government bonds with money that has been newly created by the Central Banks. Hence, the banks are in effect creating new money and pumping it into the system. Therefore, the demand for bonds that absorb this newly created money is bound to rise. It is for this reason that the quantitative easing (QE) money is used to buy only government bonds ensuring that no private parties make any profits as a result of this government policy. The US government is thus said to be having an easier time financing it is $2 billion per day debt requirement, thanks to the quantitative easing (QE) policy that it has introduced.

Bubble: When a huge amount of investments are legally designated for a single asset class, there is bound to be some sort of bubble creation. For instance, government bonds are the only asset class wherein banks can invest their newly created money. Hence, the governments have to issue more bonds and banks have to print more money to keep the system running. As such, the true financing costs of the bonds are hidden. This is because when a lot of buyers chase a limited amount of bonds, the yield of the bonds remains less.

The governments can afford to give less interest and still sell their bonds because of the increased competition amongst investors.

Speculation: The policy of quantitative easing (QE) has also led to the creation of a lot of speculative activity in the bond market. Ideally, the bond market is supposed to move based on the fundamentals which are dictated by interest rate changes. Interest rate changes are small and do not move much overnight. Hence, bond markets were once considered safe havens for investments. Debt investments would make smaller but fixed returns.

However, in the recent past, the bond market is being driven single-handedly by expectations regarding the quantitative easing (QE) policy. The interest rates have taken a backseat wherein quantitative easing (QE) is running the show. Now, the quantitative easing (QE) policy is highly unpredictable. As a result, the bond markets fluctuate wildly before any major announcements by the Fed, European Central Bank (ECB), or any other authority.

Effects of QE Tapering

Like quantitative easing (QE), quantitative easing (QE) tapering also has many effects on the market. Some of the major effects of quantitative easing (QE) tapering are as follows:

Decreased Demand: The policy of quantitative easing (QE) tapering has a completely reverse effect as compared to quantitative easing (QE). Whereas quantitative easing (QE) prompted the investors to pump in more and more money in the government bond markets because of legal compulsion, the policy of quantitative easing (QE) tapering does the exact opposite. As the news spreads that the government is not going to print any more money and invest in the market, people begin to withdraw their investments from the bond market and use the proceeds to invest in another market. The fundamentals of the market may have remained unchanged but an announcement of quantitative easing (QE) tapering is enough to create a significant dent in the market.

Yields Rise: The policy of quantitative easing (QE) in a way subsidizes the cost of issuing bonds for the government. It does so by creating excess demand which creates competition amongst investors. When the policy of quantitative easing (QE) tapering is implemented, the exact opposite happens. This means that the investors leave the markets in huge numbers. As such the yields suddenly spike up causing the prices of the bonds to soar exponentially.

Bubble Burst: Thus, the policy of quantitative easing (QE) leads to the creation of a bubble whereas the policy of quantitative easing (QE) tapering leads to the bursting of that very same bubble. The bonds have an intrinsic value of let's say X dollars. During the quantitative easing (QE) period, excess demand raises the value to X+5 dollars and sustains it there further perpetuating the bubble. When quantitative easing (QE) tapering is implemented, the value drops to X-5 dollars. Hence, the stability of the bond markets is jeopardized by the booms and busts created by the quantitative easing (QE) policy.

Quantitative Easing and Gold

The policy of quantitative easing (QE) affects almost every single market in the world. The modern-day financial markets are so interconnected that a change in one market is reflected in the other markets too. Hence, along with bond and stock markets, quantitative easing (QE) creates waves in the gold market too. To many, this may seem to be surprised as to what does a precious metal like gold has to do with government policies! Well, it turns out that gold and government policy have been around for centuries. The effect of quantitative easing (QE) is therefore only one of the latest of many government policies which have affected the gold market. In this article, we will try and explain the link between gold and fiat money as well as how quantitative easing (QE) affects both of them.

Gold Vs Paper Money

The modern monetary system is a competition between paper money and gold which was the money of ancient times. Earlier money used to be printed only if there was sufficient gold in reserve to be able to print that money. However, the world has moved to a fiat money system in the 1970s when President Nixon took the world off the gold standard. Hence, there is direct competition between paper money assets and real assets such as gold. Therefore, when the demand for one goes up, the demand for the other goes down and so their prices move inversely as well because of this competition.

This up and down movement of gold and fiat currency has been further exaggerated by the quantitative easing (QE) policies being followed by the current United States government. The government artificially manipulates the money supply in the system. Therefore, it also implicitly manipulates the value and price of gold.

we will have a closer look at how the policy of quantitative easing (QE) affects the price of gold in the system.

Gold and Crisis

Gold has always been considered to be the real money by conservative investors worldwide. This is because whenever the fiat money system completely breaks down gold is what the monetary system automatically resorts to. This is what has happened in countries like Zimbabwe when the system completely collapsed. Hence, whenever, there is speculation regarding the breakdown of the monetary system due to hyperinflation, gold prices will move in the upwards direction. This is what happened when the subprime mortgage bubble burst in 2008. There was fear that the entire economy will go under and therefore the investors rushed to buy as much gold as they possibly could.

Hence the demand for gold increases during a crisis. It is widely believed that the current standards of quantitative easing (QE) will end up in a crisis. This is because the current standards of quantitative easing (QE) cannot be sustained. Hence, the demand for gold, as well as the gold price, is expected to skyrocket shortly as and when quantitative easing (QE) tapering begins.

Excess Money and Gold

Excess money in the system makes it appear that the price of gold is actually rising. In reality, this is not the case. Consider the fact that a rising tide raises all ships. Therefore, when the Fed creates new money and injects it into the system, the prices of everything go up. However, the prices of gold go up comparatively less than the prices of other paper assets like stocks and bonds.

Hence it appears as if the prices of gold are increasing in nominal terms. However, when we consider the same in real terms i.e. in comparison to other assets, the price of gold usually declines in a period when excessive quantitative easing takes place.

Quantitative Easing (QE) Tapering and Gold

The mere news of quantitative easing (QE) tapering brings shockwaves to the gold market. In the recent past, whenever the Fed has so much as hinted towards using the policy of quantitative easing (QE) tapering, the prices of gold have skyrocketed overnight.

This is because quantitative easing (QE) tapering means that the Fed will stop the excess money creation that it is doing now. Hence, there will be fewer dollars in the system chasing the same amount of gold. Fewer dollars would imply that the real value of gold will rise much faster than the nominal value. Hence, quantitative easing (QE) tapering makes it look like gold as an asset class is appreciating in terms of nominal value. However, the actual appreciation comes in terms of real value.

There have also been rumors that Central Banks around the world have been leasing out gold in the markets. As such they may not have possession of the amount of gold on hand as they claim to do. Therefore, the markets may be hit by a double whammy of contraction in the money supply and a sudden perceived shortage of the amount of gold in the world. This double whammy may be enough to spike the price of gold to historic levels.

There are some conservative investors like Peter Schiff who believe that gold is the future and that one must invest as much in gold as one possibly can. Their views are further supported by how the markets react to the quantitative easing (QE) tapering policies.

Quantitative Easing and the Forex Market

The policy of quantitative easing (QE) and quantitative easing (QE) tapering affects many markets worldwide. One of these markets is the Forex market. In 2012, the mere news of a possible quantitative easing (QE) tapering by the Fed sent the world currency markets into a tailspin as many other currencies belonging to the developing countries (with huge fiscal deficits) faced historic lows against the dollar.

The cause and effect relationship between the quantitative easing (QE) tapering policy and the Forex market is unclear. However, the fact that such a relationship exists is certain. In this article, we will explore this relationship in more detail.

A Fresh Look at the Forex Rate

There are a lot of explanations given as to what Forex rates are and what do they represent. Some of these explanations include increasingly complex theories about the functioning of the Forex market. However, for our purpose, we will take a fresh new, and simple look at the Forex markets.

So what is it that sets the Forex rates between any two currencies? How does the market determine that $1 equals 65 Rupees? The answers may sound complex but they all point out the same thing. The market expects that in the future there will be 65 rupees in circulation for every dollar that is in circulation. The keyword here is future expectations, not the present condition. At the present, there may be more or less than 65 rupees for every dollar. However, the market factors in the current news and creates a price that represents a future valuation. The Forex rate is therefore nothing but an expected ratio between the two currencies at a future date.

QE and the Forex Rates

The above being said the quantitative easing (QE) policy can and does therefore have a profound effect on the Forex rates. This is because when quantitative easing (QE) takes place the government of one country unilaterally decided to increase or decrease the number of its currency units. This increase or decrease affects the ratio of that currency to other currencies in the market. Usually, when the government follows the policy of quantitative easing (QE), it increases the money supply by creating a new currency and pumping the same into the bond markets.

For instance, when the US implemented the policy of quantitative easing (QE), it created billions of dollars and used them to buy troubled real estate assets as well as government bonds. However, the total number of dollars in circulation went up by billions of units. Therefore, the price and the purchasing power of the dollar in the Forex market are bound to fall unless the policy of quantitative easing (QE) is also used by other economies.

For instance, if both US and Europe are using quantitative easing (QE) then the currency pair of US/EUR may not fluctuate highly in value because the fall in the value of the dollar may be more or less offset by the fall in the value of the Euro and the effects may nullify each other.

However, if the US adopts the policy of quantitative easing (QE) and India does not, then, in that case, the number of dollars in circulation will increase but the number of rupees will not. Therefore, the US dollar will lose its purchasing power relative to the rupee and this will reflect in the Forex market via dropped prices.

QE Tapering and the Forex Rates

The policy of quantitative easing (QE) tapering has the exact opposite effect as compared to the policy of quantitative easing (QE). Quantitative easing (QE) tapering creates a situation wherein the speed at which new money was being supplied into the economy is reduced.

Therefore, if the US announces the policy of quantitative easing (QE) tapering today, the markets assume that the US will reduce the rate at which new money is being created. Therefore, the number of dollars that will be available for circulation in the market at a later date will be less than expected. Now, here too, there can be multiple scenarios.

If the US and Europe were to simultaneously announce the policy of quantitative easing (QE) tapering with about the same degree of magnitude, the Forex prices between these two currencies may not fluctuate that much.

On the other hand, if one of these countries were to announce the policy of quantitative easing (QE) tapering whereas the policies of the other remain unchanged, then the quantitative easing (QE) tapering would have a severe impact on the Forex rates between the given currency pair.

Impact on the Markets

Financial markets do not operate in a vacuum. This is truer of Forex markets which operate on a 24 by 7 basis worldwide. Therefore, even if multiple central banks were to implement the quantitative easing (QE) tapering policy in conjunction with each other, they would still end up creating ripple effects in the markets. They may be able to minimize or negate the effects between their currency pairs. However, the Forex market as a whole may face severe consequences. Many analysts believe that the almost certain event of quantitative easing (QE) tapering in the near future will wreck havoc in the Forex markets apart from many other asset markets in the world.

Quantitative Easing and Interest Rates

Quantitative Easing (QE) impacts almost every market in the globe. This is because it impacts certain fundamental economic factors which are interconnected across the world. One such factor is interest rates. The policy of Quantitative Easing (QE) is capable of significantly impacting interest rates in various ways. Since interest rates can change the market overnight, Quantitative Easing (QE) has the inherent potential to change global markets overnight. In this article, we will look at the short term, medium-term, and long term impacts of Quantitative Easing (QE).

How Quantitative Easing (QE) and Interest Rates Interact?

Quantitative Easing (QE) has a profound effect on the interest rates that are prevalent in the economy. It may be used by Fed as an alternative to the interest rate policy. However, in the end, it ends up influencing the interest rates even more. The interaction between the Quantitative Easing (QE) policy and the interest rates is said to be fairly simple. At first, the Quantitative Easing (QE) policy leads to a reduction in the interest rates i.e. in the short and medium-term, the interest rates go down. However, in the long term, the interest rates go up significantly. For our purpose, the long term may be defined as a period of 5 years or more. This is because Quantitative Easing (QE) is a relatively nascent form of fiscal policy and its long-term effects can only be theoretically calculated. There isn't much empirical evidence to base the hypotheses on.

The following are the reasons that Quantitative Easing (QE) causes interest rates to drop in the short and medium-term and move up in the long term. The first two reasons explain the drop in the interest rates whereas the third reason explains the rise in the interest rates at a later date.

208

Indirect Signals

Central Banks usually adopt a Quantitative Easing (QE) policy only after they have exhausted the other options. This means that Quantitative Easing (QE) is only used when the interest rates are already close to zero and cannot be dropped much further. In such a situation, the market participants have two kinds of anticipations. The first one is that the government will leave the interest rates untouched whereas the other expectation is that the Central Bank may raise the interest rate.

So, when the central bank adopts the policy of Quantitative Easing (QE), they are sending indirect signals to the market that they are still in the expansionary phase. This means that there is almost no chance that they will raise the interest rates in the short term. As a result, the short-term interest rates continue to fall further or stay stagnant since there is almost no chance that the central bank may raise it further.

Liquidity Premium

The bonds being sold by the banks and private parties have a liquidity premium attached to their cost. This is because these bonds have an active secondary market wherein they can be liquidated i.e. converted to cash at any given point in time. The amount of liquidity in these markets depends upon the amount of cash that is available in the system relative to the number of securities that are present in the market. Hence if there are more bonds in the system and there is less cash to buy them, then there is less liquidity. Hence, the liquidity premium charged will be high. On the other hand, if there is more cash and fewer bonds, the liquidity premium will be less and this lesser premium will reflect in the form of reduced medium-term interest rates.

The policy of Quantitative Easing (QE) creates the second scenario i.e. a scenario wherein there are fewer bonds available in the market and more cash. This is because the central bank buys up the bonds and releases cash. Therefore the liquidity premium falls causing a drop in the medium-term interest rates.

Inflation Premium

The Quantitative Easing (QE) policy reduces the interest rates in the short and medium-term. However, in the long term, it does the exact opposite i.e. it raises the interest rates. This is because the Quantitative Easing (QE) policy is inherently expansionary. An expansionary economic policy if carried out on a longer-term basis leads to inflation in the markets. One of the fundamental purposes of the Central Banks is to keep inflation low. Hence when runaway inflation seems to become prevalent in the marketplace, the central banks are forced to raise the interest rates to bring the prices under control. Thus the expansionary policy in itself brings an end to an extended period of low-interest rates.

Therefore, over 5 years or so, the policy of Quantitative Easing (QE) will always cause the interest rates to bounce back higher than they already were.

How Quantitative Easing (QE) Tapering and Interest Rates Interact?

In the above paragraph, we saw how the policy of Quantitative Easing (QE) in itself brings about its end. However, sometimes Central Banks bring about an abrupt termination of the Quantitative Easing (QE) policy with a counter policy known as Quantitative Easing (QE) tapering.

In this case, the interest rates spike almost immediately. The market is in a state of panic because of the sudden shift of policy by the Central Bank from expansion to contraction. This knee-jerk reaction causes the markets to short stay in a state of disequilibrium wherein the interest rates go sky high before the panic settles and the interest rates return to normal which is slightly higher than they were during the Quantitative Easing (QE) period.

The policy of Quantitative Easing (QE) therefore has profound impacts on the interest rates. Since interest rates affect almost everything from corporate borrowings to derivative settlements, this policy assumes significance since it can significantly affect the economy.

Alternatives to Quantitative Easing

The Fed and the United States government have chosen the Quantitative Easing (QE) policy as the best policy to overcome the 2008 crisis. This means that there were other policies in consideration. These policies were alternatives to Quantitative Easing (QE) policy and were capable of providing a similar effect. However, the average person is not even aware of most of these policies. In this article, we have therefore decided to discuss some of these policies and their advantages and disadvantages relative to Quantitative Easing (QE). Some of the alternative policies are as follows:

Helicopter Drop

One of the alternatives to Quantitative Easing (QE) suggested by many critics is the "helicopter drop" policy. This policy is a fictional policy that was made popular by Milton Friedman. The policy is based on the assumption that a helicopter flies across various neighborhoods in the city and drops money to the people. Simply put this means that the government creates more money and distributes it to the people. This policy would also have a similar effect as Quantitative Easing (QE). This is because as and when people get their hands on the newly created money, they would start to spend it. As a result, the demands for goods and services will increase and the economy as a whole will be stimulated.

Critics argue that this policy is much better than Quantitative Easing (QE) and that the government should simply give away money to the people. This is because the helicopter drop would create a somewhat equitable distribution of money in the economy and everyone receiving the money would be better or worse off to a similar extent. However, in the case of Quantitative Easing (QE), the banks are the ones that receive the money first. As a result, they get maximum advantage out of the money which is then lent out to the people much later, and by the time the average person gets their hand on the money, inflation has already caught up!

Tax Rebates

Many economists believe that tax rebates would be a much better alternative to Quantitative Easing (QE). This is because Quantitative Easing (QE) emphasizes creating more borrowing in the economy. The borrowing may be for a productive purpose, such as setting up an industry. Alternatively, it could be for a consumption-driven purpose. Quantitative Easing (QE) does not distinguish between these two types of lending. Hence, the policy of Quantitative Easing (QE) is faulty to these economists.

Tax rebates on the other hand can be used to control, exactly who gets the additional money. For instance, the United States government could cut taxes for productive purposes. This would leave more money in the hands of the entrepreneurs who would then want to invest this money to grow their business and stimulate the economy in the process. Personal income taxes can be dropped at a lower rate to fuel the consumption of these additional goods. Tax rebates, therefore have the power of directing the newly created money to its appropriate destination.

Lower Borrowing Rates

The Quantitative Easing (QE) policy is aimed at stimulating borrowing and lending in the economy. The central bank provides the banks with excess reserves based on which they can create more loans in the open market. Theoretically, therefore a lowered interest rate would work in the same way as a Quantitative Easing (QE) policy would. However, in reality, lower interest rates do not work as well. This is because lower interest rates and other lax lending standards attract borrowers that the banks do not want to lend money. The borrowers that banks are in fact interested in lending money to are often disinterested in these interest rate gimmicks.

Deficit Spending

Another popular measure commonly used by Central Banks and governments worldwide instead of austerity is deficit spending. Under this policy, the government is advised to undertake long-term infrastructure projects in the economy. Since the government does not have the money to finance these projects, they are advised to create this money or use debt financing. In either case, the money supply of the local economy increases and the overall effect is like that of Quantitative Easing (QE). This policy has been widely used by many governments across the world. This is because it gives governments the power to redirect the resources strategically as and when required. Deficit spending, however, creates the problem of huge interest burdens if the policy is not implemented carefully. Deficit spending programs gone awry have been the cause of many bailouts around the world.

Austerity

One of the most painful alternatives to Quantitative Easing (QE) is austerity. Quantitative Easing (QE) and all the other policies listed above are aimed at providing temporary relief to the economy and the people. Long-term relief can only be achieved by undoing the wrongs of the past. As a result, austerity is the ideal solution. Sooner or later, any economy that is using Quantitative Easing (QE) will have to use austerity as well. However, most economies want to avoid that day for as long as possible. However, it must be noted that austerity is the only real solution, one that solves the problem from its root cause. It is unlike other quick-fix band-aids that are usually used by the Central Banks and governments as populist measures.

Many critics believe that Quantitative Easing (QE) was not the best choice for any of the developed nations to come out of the crisis. However, all the nations have made a unanimous choice. The results of this choice will be visible over the next few years.

Effect of Quantitative Easing on Emerging Markets

The average person believes that Quantitative Easing (QE) is a policy being implemented in developed nations like the United States, Europe, the United Kingdom, and Japan. They believe that the average person sitting in developing economies where

Quantitative Easing (QE) is not being implemented has very little to gain or lose from this policy. However, this is not true. The Quantitative Easing (QE) policy has a huge impact on the economies of emerging markets across the globe. In this article, we will trace the flow of how an issue about the solvency of developed nations is causing boom-bust cycles across the globe.

Abnormal Inflows

Quantitative Easing (QE) involves the government creating new money and using it to invest in various securities. The securities that were commonly used by the Fed i.e. the Central Bank of United States were agency securities, asset-backed securities, and treasury securities. Now, there are a limited amount of these securities. The investments in these securities were earlier driven by private investors. However, after the Quantitative Easing (QE) policy has come into existence, these securities have become the exclusive investment avenues for the government.

The private investors have therefore been looking for newer and more profitable avenues to park their investments. It is a result of this policy that the economies of emerging markets have boomed during this period of Quantitative Easing (QE). Private portfolio investors suddenly found that they have limited avenues to invest in the United States. As a result, they started looking out to other countries. Some countries like Brazil, Russia, India, China, and South Africa had relatively strong fundamentals. Therefore, investors started pumping in unheard amounts of money in this market. As a result, the stock markets and the economies of these nations underwent a boom during the Quantitative Easing (QE) period. Even now, the mere news of a Quantitative Easing (QE) tapering sends shockwaves in the markets of these economies.

Interest Rates

The interest rates of an economy are determined based on the demand and supply of money in that economy. If the demand outstrips the supply the interest rates rise and the opposite happens when supply outstrips demand. In the case of Quantitative Easing (QE), the economies of these nations suddenly found themselves flooded with money. The corporations as well as private individuals in emerging markets had access to a large amount of cash at their disposal. Therefore, the interest rates in these economies have seen a downward trend and the amount of money being lent out has gone up significantly.

Inflation

Inflation is a natural consequence if a lot of money flows in any economy and the interest rates are set low. However, in the case of emerging economies, a lot of inflation has found its way to asset prices. The inflation related to commodities such as food which form a part of the day-to-day survival has been relatively less. This is because the investors have sent their money to emerging markets from an investment point of view. Their money is therefore invested in stocks, bonds, and real estate markets of the emerging economies. Hence, emerging economies all over the world have seen an unprecedented asset price boom during the Quantitative Easing (QE) period. Many experts believe that this is just a bubble that will burst as soon as Fed introduces the Quantitative Easing (QE) tapering policy. Therefore, according to them, it is only a matter of time before the bubble bursts.

Dollar Depreciation

The Quantitative Easing (QE) policy adopted by the United States has caused the exports in the emerging economy to grow exponentially. This is because more and more dollars are leaving the United States. As such more dollars are being sold in the Forex markets. Therefore the price of the dollar relative to other currencies is rising. As a result, Americans can afford to buy more products on the international market because the dollar has a higher purchasing power. The Quantitative Easing (QE) policy is therefore creating a scenario wherein the emerging markets can perpetually export and the United States can perpetually import goods without any consequences until the policy is changed! The news of Quantitative Easing (QE) tapering is therefore bad news for emerging markets. This is because Quantitative Easing (QE) tapering may hit their exports, therefore their corporations, stock markets, and the entire economy will feel its negative effect.

Central Banks in Action

Countries like India have faced the wrath of the markets when there were expectations that the United States will adopt the policy of Quantitative Easing (QE) tapering. The rupee hit its historic low against the dollar for several consecutive days as there was an unprecedented flight of capital outside the Indian economy.

If the markets were left to their own devices, greed and panic would have overtaken the markets. As such, the rupee would have been hammered down even further by speculators looking to make a quick buck. However, the Reserve Bank of India prevented this from happening. The Reserve Bank started buying rupees and selling dollars in the market to counteract the excess supply of rupees and the shortage of dollars. The Reserve Bank had to undertake extensive transactions and even book losses to ensure that the rupee is within acceptable limits of the dollar. Hence, the policy of Quantitative Easing (QE) adversely affects the economies of emerging nations. Sometimes the issue becomes so severe that Central Banks have to come into action to prevent further damages!

Impact of Quantitative Easing Tapering on Various Stakeholders

The Quantitative Easing (QE) policy has impacted the lives of pretty much everybody on this planet. The reverse policy of Quantitative Easing (QE) tapering is also expected to have a similarly wide range effect on the lives of millions of people. Some of them may be positively affected by the Quantitative Easing (QE) tapering policy whereas others may be negatively affected by the same. In this article, we have listed down the major stakeholders who are expected to be affected by Quantitative Easing (QE) tapering and have provided a brief list of the impact that they are likely to face.

United States Government

The United States government will be one of the most impacted parties in case the Fed decides to taper its Quantitative Easing (QE) program. This is because the government is perpetually in debt and of late has found out that the demand for its bonds is weakening because of its poor economic fundamentals. Therefore, for the past few years, the Quantitative Easing (QE) program has quite literally sustained the spending binge that the US government is on. Therefore, if the Quantitative Easing (QE) program is tapered by the Fed, the government may find itself short of lenders. As a result, they may have to pay a higher yield on their debt or may have to cut down the scale of their debt issue.

United States Taxpayers

The next most affected stakeholder would be the United States taxpayers. The United States taxpayer has been funding this multibillion-dollar Quantitative Easing (QE) program ever since it started. When the government creates new money to buy these bonds, it is taking away a certain portion of the value of the existing money. The new money derives its value from the loss of value of the old money. Hence, the taxpayers and pretty much anyone holding a dollar bill are at a loss when Quantitative Easing (QE) programs are announced. Therefore when the Quantitative Easing (QE) program is tapered, the United States taxpayers will heave a sigh of relief as the plundering of their wealth through official means will come to an end.

United States Investors

The United States investors will face a number of outcomes if the Quantitative Easing (QE) program is tapered. The effects of these outcomes remain largely uncertain and any guess is considered to be nothing except speculation. However, experts have considered a wide variety of possibilities and some of the most probable ones include:

Higher cost of funding since the markets will turn bearish. Once the supply of excess money by the Fed is stopped, the base interest rates will rise. This rise in interest rates will find its way to the required rate of return on all investments, thereby simply raising the cost of capital across investment opportunities.

A large number of United States corporations make a significant chunk of their profits through their overseas subsidiaries. A lot of these subsidiaries rely on a strong dollar for demand to be created. Hence, Quantitative Easing (QE) tapering could lead to a possibility of lower earnings from foreign subsidiaries.

Lastly, the Quantitative Easing (QE) tapering is expected to create a flight of United States capital which is currently invested in foreign markets.

Geopolitical considerations following the Quantitative Easing (QE) tapering will make this flight of capital an imperative. Hence, once the Quantitative Easing (QE) tapering program is launched, investors will have to liquidate their assets at whatever prices possible and move the money back to America. This sudden sale is expected to hurt the United States investor interests. Asset Markets

All the asset markets in the world will be widely impacted by the Quantitative Easing (QE) tapering program. We have discussed the individual impacts on most of the markets in the form of individual articles in this module. However, to summarize, one can say that the asset markets of the world will see some serious "never seen before" volatility as a result of the Quantitative Easing (QE) program.

This is because fiat money is the monetary base in which the prices of everything else are calculated. Therefore, if the value of the "monetary base" changes, then the value of everything from real estate to gold also changes. There will be some serious redistribution of wealth in the markets when Quantitative Easing (QE) tapering takes place.

Foreign Investors

Foreign investors are likely to be on the winning side if Quantitative Easing (QE) tapering takes place. This is because they exchange their local currency for dollars and invest in the United States markets. One of the biggest impacts of the Quantitative Easing (QE) tapering program will be an increase in the value of the dollar. Therefore, foreign investors who have invested their money in the United States markets stand to benefit from this massive Foreign Exchange gain. A part of this gain may be offset because of the lost business as a result of economic mayhem around the world. However, the significant movement in the Forex markets is expected to more than offset the same.

Emerging Markets

The economies of the emerging markets have been booming of late. This boom has largely been constructed based on rising exports to the United States markets which are created by the Quantitative Easing (QE) policy. A reverse policy of Quantitative Easing (QE) tapering would therefore cause a sudden period of recession in these markets because of a sudden slowdown in aggregate demand.

Therefore, some people stand to gain from the Quantitative Easing (QE) tapering policy whereas others stand to lose. However, almost everyone stands to be affected.

What Does The Federal Reserve Mean When It Talks About Tapering?

In response to the economic impact of the COVID-19 pandemic, the Federal Reserve cut short-term interest rates to zero on March 15, 2020, and restarted its large-scale asset purchases (more commonly known as quantitative easing, or QE). Since July 2020, the Fed has been buying $80 billion of Treasury securities and $40 billion of agency mortgage-backed securities (MBS) each month. As the economy rebounded in mid- 2021, Fed officials began talking about slowing—or tapering—the pace of its bond purchases.

WHY DOES THE FED BUY LONG-TERM DEBT SECURITIES?

Quantitative easing helps the economy by reducing long-term interest rates (making business and mortgage borrowing cheaper) and by signaling the Fed's intention to keep using monetary policy to support the economy. The Fed turns to QE when short-term interest rates fall nearly to zero and the economy still needs help.

By buying U.S. government debt and mortgage-backed securities, the Fed reduces the supply of these bonds in the broader market. Private investors who desire to hold these securities will then bid up the prices of the remaining supply, lowering their yield. This is called the "portfolio balance" effect. This mechanism is particularly important when the Fed purchases longer-term securities during periods of crisis. Even when short-term rates have fallen to zero, long-term rates often remain above this effective lower bound, providing more space for purchases to stimulate the economy.

Lower Treasury yields are a benchmark for other private sector interest rates, such as corporate bonds and mortgages. With low rates, households are more likely to take out a mortgage or car loans, and businesses are more likely to invest in equipment and hire workers. Lower interest rates are also associated with higher asset prices, increasing the wealth of households and thus driving spending.

Bond purchases can impact market expectations about the future path of monetary policy. QE is seen as a signal from the Fed that it intends to keep interest rates low for some time. Overall, the large-scale asset purchases that took place during and after the global financial crisis had powerful effects on lowering 10- year Treasury yields.

Federal Reserve Balance Sheet: Assets

The Fed's current bond purchases differ in composition from earlier QE programs. While previous rounds of QE primarily involved the purchase of longer-term securities, the Fed is currently purchasing Treasuries across a broader range of maturities. This was driven by the Fed's original goal of calming a distressed Treasury market in March 2020.

Federal Reserve Treasury Holdings by Maturity
WHAT IS TAPERING?

Tapering is the gradual slowing of the pace of the Federal Reserve's large-scale asset purchases. Tapering does not refer to an outright reduction of the Fed's balance sheet, only to a reduction in the pace of its expansion. At some point, after tapering is complete, the central bank is likely to gradually reduce the size of its balance sheet by letting maturing securities "run-off" the balance sheet without replacing them, as it did from October 2017 until September 2019.

The Fed's motivation for tapering is to slowly remove the monetary stimulus it has been providing the economy. Specifically, according to guidance the Fed issued in December, tapering will begin when the economy has made "substantial further progress" toward its goals. Some members of the Fed's policy-setting committee, the Federal Open Market Committee (FOMC), has noted that employment remains far below the pre-pandemic level, suggesting that patience is needed. Other members have expressed concern about inflationary pressures and excessive risk-taking in financial markets as a result of the Fed's asset purchases.

The Fed has made clear that tapering will precede any increase in its target for short-term interest rates. So tapering not only reduces the amount of QE but is also seen as a forewarning of tighter monetary policy to come, as was observed in the aftermath of the Great Recession. The combination of projected reductions in asset purchases and the possibility of higher rates in 2013 led to a period of high volatility and rising rates in the bond market—an episode that became known as the taper tantrum.

WHAT WAS THE TAPER TANTRUM?

In response to the global financial crisis, the Fed began purchasing Treasury securities and mortgage-backed securities in

2009. There were three rounds of purchases dubbed QE1, QE2, and QE3. The first two were for pre-announced totals. The third, launched in September 2012, was open-ended; the Fed said it would keep buying bonds until labor market conditions improved.

In Congressional testimony on May 21, 2013, Chair Ben Bernanke gave the first public signal that a taper was on the horizon. "If we see continued improvement and we have confidence that it is going to be sustained, then we could, in the next few meetings, take a step down in our pace of purchases," he said.

Bernanke's words, apparently surprising the markets, set off an increase in market interest rates known as the taper tantrum. The bond market pushed 10-year Treasury yields up slightly, from 1.94 percent on May 21 to 2.03 percent on May 22, 2013. Following the June FOMC meeting, Bernanke elaborated on the tapering plan, and yields rose more substantially, eventually hitting 2.96 percent on September 10. This occurred despite efforts by Bernanke and other FOMC members to emphasize that any reduction in asset purchases would be gradual and that an increase in the Fed's target for short-term rates was not imminent.

The impacts of the taper tantrum on the U.S. economy were relatively mild, with the economy growing at a rate of 2.6 percent in 2013 (on a Q4/Q4 basis) despite fiscal as well as monetary tightening. But it had greater effects on financial markets abroad where the increase in Treasury yields drove capital outflows and currency depreciation, especially in emerging markets such as Brazil, India, Indonesia, South Africa, and Turkey.

In December 2013, the Fed began to taper, reducing the pace of asset purchases from $85 billion per month to $75 billion per month. Purchases were reduced by a further $10 billion at each subsequent meeting (in February 2014, Janet Yellen took over as chair). The asset purchase program ended in October

2014, and the Fed began shrinking the balance sheet in October 2017.

WHAT WILL TAPERING MEAN FOR THE TIMING OF FED RATE HIKES?

As the U.S. has begun to emerge from the COVID-19 pandemic, the economy has picked up more rapidly than initially expected, leading the Fed to consider removing some of its monetary stimuli. In June 2020, the FOMC forecast that real gross domestic product (GDP) would fall by 6.5 percent in 2020. Similarly, in July 2020, the Congressional Budget Office (CBO) projected that real GDP would fall 5.9 percent for the year. Real GDP fell by just 2.4 percent in 2020 and grew rapidly in the first two quarters of 2021. This has led the market and FOMC to evaluate the eventual tapering of asset purchases and raising of interest rates.

Distinguishing short-term interest rate policy from tapering has been a communication challenge for the Fed dating back to the taper tantrum. This time, the FOMC has repeatedly indicated that tapering will precede any consideration of rate hikes. Fed chair Jerome Powell stated in April 2021 that tapering will occur "well before the time we would consider raising rates."

HOW WILL TAPER INFLUENCE LONG¬TERM INTEREST RATES?

Tapering can impact long-term interest rates through both its direct effects on bond markets and the signal it provides about the Fed's future policy intentions.

Since tapering refers to the slowing of the Fed's bond purchases rather than the reduction of its holdings, the Fed's balance sheet is still growing, and thus the Fed is providing monetary stimulus to the economy. This could restrain any upward pressure on long-term rates from the Fed's tapering. There is evidence to support this idea: a 2013 study by Fed economists found that the size of the balance sheet is more important than the pace of purchases in lowering long-term yields.

However, long-term rates also reflect market expectations about the course of short-term rates. Since tapering can signal to markets that the Fed is shifting to a less accommodative policy stance in the future, this could lead to a rise in long-term rates as occurred during the taper tantrum.

WHAT HAS THE FED SAID ABOUT WHEN IT WILL BEGIN TAPERING?

In December 2020, the Fed said it would continue to increase its holdings of Treasury securities by at least $80 billion per month and of agency mortgage-backed securities by at least $40 billion per month "until substantial further progress has been made toward the Committee's maximum employment and price stability goals."

In June 2021, Powell acknowledged at his press conference that progress had been made toward the Fed's macroeconomic goals. The FOMC began assessing the pace and composition of its asset purchases alongside the economic conditions on a meeting-by-meeting basis in July 2021.

Minutes of the June 2021 FOMC meeting recorded some disagreement among Fed policymakers about when to begin tapering. "Various participants mentioned that they expected the conditions for beginning to reduce the pace of asset purchases to be met somewhat earlier than they had anticipated," the minutes said. Other participants, however, said that the Fed "should be patient in assessing progress toward its goals." FOMC members also discussed different speeds of tapering for Treasuries and mortgage-backed securities at the meeting. "Several participants saw benefits to reducing the pace of [MBS] purchases more quickly or earlier than Treasury purchases in light of valuation pressures in housing markets," the minutes said.

Several Fed officials have addressed the timeline for tapering more directly since the June meeting. For instance, Governor

Christopher Waller said, "I think everybody anticipates that tapering could move up earlier than when they originally thought. Whether that's this year, we'll see, but it certainly could [be]." Waller also signaled that he would prefer to taper the purchase of mortgage-backed securities before the purchases of Treasury securities. Richmond Fed President Thomas Barkin said, "It's pretty clear to me we have had substantial further progress against our inflation goal. [...] If the labor market opens as I suggested it might, then I think we're going to get there in relatively short order."

However, not all members of the FOMC believe that substantial further progress is imminent. New York Fed President John Williams said, "We set a very clear marker, I think, not a quantitative marker, but a very clear marker that we want substantial further progress relative to where we were. That's where I'm focused, clearly right now we have not achieved that."

Market analysts adjusted expectations after the June FOMC meeting, predicting the Fed would announce its plan for tapering in the fall, which implies that tapering would start around the beginning of 2022.

CONCLUSION

The IMF would allocate SDRs counter-cyclically and treat them as deposits of countries, which could be used in lending to them. This would be valid even though SDRs are confined to act as a means of payment only among central banks and not private agents. Reforming the system in this way would be effective in addressing some of the core imperfections of the current global monetary system. Developing countries, in particular, would benefit from this reform given that they would receive part of the seigniorage related to global monetary creation, and that their balance of payments needs require them to use their SDR allocations more frequently.

In the initial stages of reform, it is important to promote the SDRs only as a reserve asset and not as an international means of payment, which would be costly for the US economy. This would make the reform more politically feasible. This is also in the long-term interest of the U.S. given the gradual erosion of confidence in the dollar as a reserve currency and the risk of losing monetary policy autonomy. For the developing countries holding dollar reserves, the costs of transition to an SDR-based system would be lower than the cost of dollar depreciation if they exchange their reserves for SDRs through a substitution account. In the medium run, new SDR allocations would allow developing countries to share in the seigniorage resulting from reserve creation and lower the cost of borrowing international reserves.